Ulster Local Studies

Journal of the Federation for
Ulster Local Studies

Ulster Local Studies is published twice yearly, summer and winter. It aims to carry out the objects of the Federation as laid down in the Constitution:

1. To promote the study and recording of the history, antiquities, and folk-life of Ulster.

2. To encourage the provision of the necessary services for the furtherance of those local historical studies in Ulster.

3. To develop communication and co-operation —

   (a) among voluntary associations concerned with local historical studies in Ulster; and

   (b) between these associations and other relevant organisations, statutory and voluntary.

Additional copies of the **journal may be ordered** from:—

> The Federation for Ulster Local Studies,
> Institute of Irish Studies,
> 8 Fitzwilliam Street,
> Belfast BT9 6AW.
> (Tel/Fax: 0232 235254)
> at a cost of £2.75 (incl. p & p) per copy.

Editorial correspondence, books for review and all communications in connection with the Federation should be sent to the above address.

Volume 14 No. 2   Winter 1992

Editorial Board

Contributors

Professor John H. Andrews is a noted geographer and author of *A Paper Landscape: the Ordnance Survey in Nineteenth Century Ireland.*

John B. Cunningham is a well-known writer and lecturer in local history. He is headmaster of St. Davog's Primary School, Belleek and a member of the Federation's Executive Committee.

Annesley J. Malley is a Chartered Surveyor and Land Agent. He is a member of the North West Archaeological and Historical Society and a member of the Federation's Townlands sub-committee.

Sam Gray is Mapping and Charts Officer with the Ordnance Survey of Northern Ireland.

Eull Dunlop is a teacher at Cambridge House Boys Grammar School and Secretary of the Mid-Antrim Historical Group.

Art J. Hughes is a researcher with the Ulster Place-names Research Project based at Queen's University, Belfast.

Trevor J. Parkhill is Principal Records Officer at the Public Record Office of Northern Ireland.

Kathleen Gormley is a member of the North West Archaeological and Historical Society and Honorary Secretary of the Federation.

Contents

Foreword

On the two hundredth anniversary of its foundation, it was timely that the Ordnance Survey (OS) should be the subject of the 1991 seminar of the Federation for Ulster Local Studies. Those who travelled to Lisnarick in Fermanagh for this event returned home with an enhanced awareness of the role of the OS in our local history. The interplay between the OS and the local historian in Ulster is further examined in this volume, which includes some of the papers presented at the Fermanagh seminar.

It is my hope that this book will bring home to its readers the cultural dimension of the OS as well as its undoubted technical expertise. Not only, have the maps of the OS been consistently produced to the highest standards of surveying, but in the nineteenth century, the OS was in part instrumental in the study of placenames in Ireland; a subject which to this day fascinates many local historians. Thus, two of the foremost pioneers in the study of townlands are featured in this volume: John O'Donovan, whose travels, observations and recordings of native lore and derivations have been of lasting value and Bishop William Reeves, an ecclesiastical gentleman with strong Ulster links, whose scholarship remains in many ways unchallenged today.

On behalf of the Publications Committee of the Federation for Ulster Local Studies, I wish to place on record my thanks to those who have contributed to this volume and to Mr. Tony Canavan and Miss Janet McMaw who have so expertly brought this volume to fruition.

R.H. Foy
Chairman
Publications Committee

'More suitable to the English tongue' :
The cartography of Celtic placenames[1]

J.H. Andrews

My subject is the language of maps, and I use this phrase in a literally literal sense: by language I simply mean words composed of letters from the roman alphabet. For purposes of definition, I shall identify the language of a map not from its name but from the words of it that are not names, words like 'north', 'scale', and so on. In this sense there are so few early Celtic-language maps that in an hour's lecture we can reasonably ignore them and concentrate entirely on English-language maps of the Celtic countries, and particularly of Ireland, though most of what I have to say is equally applicable to Gaelic Scotland, and some of it at least is equally applicable to Wales.

There is another preliminary warning that occurred to me during Graham Clark's lecture on 'The cartouche as a cultural icon: the American experience' (January 1992). He equated the imperialistic symbolism of cartouches in maps of America during the colonial period with the use of English placenames for early colonial habitations. What he did not say was that the cartouches were devised by mapmakers while the names had presumably been conferred by settlers who were not mapmakers. But for some of us this vocational difference is worth keeping in mind. For me, at least, the interest of map-history lies in what makes a cartographer different from other people. I don't want a map-historian to tell me what people in general are like. I already know what they are like. It's true that having said that, I shall now spend a great deal of time discussing the use of placenames by people in general, but this is only as a long build-up to a strictly cartographic punch-line.

One difference between mapmakers and other people who have occasion to write down placenames is that mapmakers (despite their poor reputation in this respect) are more conscientious. And here we must switch momentarily from a literal to a metaphorical interpretation of language. Most verbal sentences containing placenames are statements about places, with the name functioning simply as a means to an end. But many cartographic sentences, as we might figuratively call maps or parts of maps, are statements about the names on those maps: what they are saying is that 'so-and-so' (as it were in inverted commas) is the name of such and such a place. Which means that cartographers have to think about names in a way that other people usually find unnecessary. But my first major point is that whatever may have happened in America or elsewhere, in the Celtic world this extra care and attention have never had the slightest influence on the general public. Lately the cartographic profession has come under some heavy criticism: Anglo-Irish cartographers may have been as wicked as any others, but at least they were harmlessly wicked.

This public indifference emerges most clearly on the very few occasions when a cartographer has invented a new name in Ireland or a new way of spelling an old name. Take for instance the country's largest lake, Lough Neagh. This has been renamed twice by map-makers. But the users of maps have never abandoned 'Lough Neagh' in favour of its other proposed names, 'Lough Sidney' and 'Lough Chichester', even though Henry Sidney and Arthur Chichester were each in their day the most powerful man in Ireland. The truth is that if public recognition depended on cartographers, St. Patrick himself would still be a nonentity. We know this because in the 1890s the hydrographer to the Royal Navy had no success whatever when he proposed the new name 'St. Patrick's Channel' for part of the Irish Sea.

As the following examples suggest, the majority of written placenames seem to pass through two historical stages, experimentation and consolidation, the stage of consolidation being reached when a majority of educated opinion agrees how a name should be spelt and pronounced.

Some cartographers' spellings of Irish placenames

[*Loch*] *nEathach*. 1558 Arke; 1563 Eagh; 1567 Niaghe; 1580 Eaugh; 1580 Eaghe; 1580 Eagh; 1590 Eaugh; 1602 Neagh or Euagh; 1603 Eaghe; 1610 Eagh; 1610 Eaugh; 1659, 1685, 1700, 1708, 1760, 1777, 1780, 1785, 1792, 1795, 1811, 1818, 1833 (OS), 1839 NEAGH.

Beal Atha Seanaidh. 1563 Balashenan; 1571 B.Shenen; 1580 Balleshenin; 1590 B.Shenen; 1597 B.Shanon; 1599 B. Shenan; 1610 Ballyshenan; 1685 Ballishanon; 1700 Ballyshanon; 1700, 1708, 1760, 1776, 1777, 1785, 1792, 1795, 1811, 1818, 1836 (OS), 1839 BALLYSHANNON.

Inis Ceithleann. 1580 Inneskelly; 1599 Eniskelin; 1602 Eniskillin; 1610 Iniskillin; 1685 Eniskelling; 1700 Eniskilling; 1708, 1760, 1776 Enniskilling; 1777, 1785, 1792, 1795, 1811, 1818, 1835 (OS), 1839 ENNISKILLEN.

Geisell. 1564 Geshyll; 1571 Ghessell; 1610 Ghesell; 1685 Geshill; 1708 Gashill; 1777, 1785 Geashill; 1792 Geshil; 1811 Geshill; 1818 Geashill; 1839 Geashil; 1840 GEASHILL (OS).

The exact chronology of this sequence obviously varies from one name to another, but for many Irish names a period of experimentation was completed in the course of the eighteenth century – before the time of the Ordnance Survey, to emphasise a rather obvious point whose significance will emerge later. The second period, of consolidation, will be arbitrarily terminated for the purposes of this talk at around 1850. In maps of Ireland both these periods are well represented, because here, as in various other European countries, maps become numerous in the middle of the sixteenth century and I need hardly tell you that most of them were associated with the conquest of Ireland by the English. General discussions of the country's placenames are a later development, beginning in 1665 with an act of the Irish parliament known as the Act of Explanation, which among many other provisions authorised landowners in Ireland to find names 'more suitable to the English tongue' than the allegedly 'barbarous and uncouth' names in general use, the phrase 'barbarous and uncouth' being glossed by a knowledgeable commentator of the time, Dr. William Petty, with the additional word 'unintelligible'. I've already mentioned Irish people's indifference to maps. A better-known national characteristic is their indifference to acts of parliament. After 1665 they all went on using the same kind of name that they had used before, couth or uncouth.

But for us the Act of Explanation is still a useful jumping-off point. Of course the Dublin parliament of Charles II was essentially a mouthpiece of English opinion, and you may regard this particular statute as an unusually frank statement of English contempt for what was then Ireland's most widely spoken language, contempt which a puppet government apparently hoped to express by robbing a downtrodden majority of that majority's rightful toponymic inheritance. But were such words as 'barbarous', 'uncouth' and 'unintelligible' really being directed at the Irish language? Let me propose an alternative hypothesis, starting with another question. Why should a seventeenth-century Englishman expect any placename to be intelligible? Most of his own names, from 'London' downwards, were composed of meaningless syllables in meaningless combinations. Connotative or dictionary names, like 'Red-hill' or 'New-castle', were comparatively rare in England, as they were in many continental countries. But (as Mary Pedley of the William L. Clements Library, Ann Arbor, has kindly told me) when the French government's surveyors reached Britanny in the 1770s they were particularly advised to study the meanings of that province's Celtic names.

9

So there is my second major point: most Celtic placenames do have meanings. One of the first English cartographers to acknowledge this as any kind of peculiarity was Aaron Arrowsmith in his *Memoir relative to the construction of the map of Scotland* (1809). In England, Arrowsmith advised, cartographers should follow the customary spelling; in Scotland they would be justified in consulting Gaelic etymology. The reason for the greater preponderance of connotative names in Celtic countries is presumably that the Celtic languages have changed less, since medieval times, than the English language. And there is one interesting result of this difference that seems seldom to have attracted comment. Among the various nations of the British Isles the one people who have lost their toponymic inheritance are the English, a calamity most of them have somehow managed to endure with uncomplaining fortitude.

But to return to the Act of Explanation: as the following random sample shows, what the Irish parliament confronted in 1665 was an equation with three terms.

Irish forms	English forms	Forms commonly used
Ath-na-riogh	Kings' Ford	Athenry
Cluain-fhada	Long Meadow	Clonad
Cill-a-mhuilinn	Mill Church	Killawillin
Druim-dubh	Black Ridge	Drumduff
Leamhchoill	Elm Wood	Laughil
Muigh-iseal	Low Plain	Myshall
Sradbhaile	Street Town	Stradbally
Tulaigh-ban	White Hill	Tullybane

Thus a typical Irish name with nothing uncouth about it was 'Muine Beag', which translates into the equally unobjectionable English name of 'Little Thicket'. The third and much the most familiar term in this equation is 'Moneybeg', and this is where the barbarity and uncouthness come in because 'Moneybeg' belongs to no language and means nothing. The same kind of triplication appears in many other names, for instance Brian Friel's 'Baile Beag' (Irish) with its alternatives 'Little Town' (English) and 'Ballybeg' (barbarous and uncouth). To elucidate these variations we must next distinguish five sources of toponymic change: substitution, translation, transcription, dictation, and restoration; and I shall now say something about each of these processes in turn, bearing in mind that more than one process may contribute to the history of a single name.

Naked cultural imperialism is best represented by substitution, which means the replacement of a native name by a completely different English name, as when Moneybeg was rechristened 'Bagenalstown' after being taken over by the Bagenal family in the seventeenth century. Ireland has witnessed many such substitutions, but most of them were quite unconnected with cartography; indeed most of them occurred at a time when, to judge from Professor P.D.A. Harvey's *History of topographical maps*, there was no such thing as cartography in Ireland. When English mapmakers did take the field they very seldom invented totally new English names like 'Sidney' or 'Chichester'. Like most of their colleagues outside Ireland in similar historical circumstances they were too busy surveying the world to have much time for remaking it; and they knew that to change the name of a village was no more part of their professional duty than demolishing the village and rebuilding it somewhere else. This self-effacing modesty is well personified by the otherwise not particularly self-effacing economist, statistician, and expert on Irish affairs, William Petty. Petty was a strong believer in anglicisation for placenames and for everything else in Ireland. As official surveyor of forfeited estates in the 1650s he also happened to be the most prolific of all Ireland's pre-Ordnance Survey cartographers, with a through-put of names that has been estimated at 25,000. Yet Petty is not known ever to have replaced an old Irish name with a new English name of his own invention.

So much for our verdict of not guilty on the charge of substitution. Our second process, translation, has recently become a metaphor symbolising all the cultural mischief done by Englishmen in Ireland, though, oddly enough, outside the domain of this metaphor translation is everywhere accepted as a form of recognition and acknowledgement: we show our respect for a writer by translating him. In fact there is even less cartographic evidence for translation in Ireland than for substitution. And in general, it is easy to demonstrate the inefficacy of both these processes among cartographers and non-cartographers alike. Of the names current in Ireland today, whether on or off the map, more than ninety per cent are still unmistakably of Celtic origin. This is in a country where the overwhelming majority of people now habitually speak English. So, once again, recent opinion is wide of the mark. Yes, Saxon did prevail over Celt in Ireland, linguistically and in other ways. But placenames do less than anything else in the Irishman's vocabulary to commemorate his defeat.

11

Transcription for the purposes of this lecture is what happens when an English-speaking writer copies a name from a Celtic-language document. Before the nineteenth century this practice seems to have been even less common in Ireland than either substitution or translation. In even a small sample of transcribed Irish names, the transcription process would soon betray itself by letters or sequences of letters which are familiar in written Irish but which in English have no audible or visible counterpart. Examples are the aspirated consonants 'b', 'd' and 'm', as represented in Irish script either by adding an 'h' to the letter in question or by crowning it with a large dot. Other Irish combinations unfamiliar in English are initial 'sr' and initial 'ts'. Comparable cases in Wales are initial double 'l' as in 'Llandudno' and initial 'Y' when followed immediately by a consonant as in 'Yspytty'. And here is an interesting difference between these two Celtic countries. The Welsh forms I have just mentioned occur throughout the maps of Christopher Saxton (1573-9) and John Speed (1610). But until the late eighteenth century such tell-tale non-English letter-sequences never occur in maps in Ireland. This is because very few people had ever seen them.

The proportion of Irish placenames that were written down in Irish-language documents before the coming of the Ordnance Survey was apparently quite small; so small that even with the whole of Irish literature at his disposal an early cartographer would still have had to draw most of his Irish-language names from unwritten sources. And of course no cartographer ever did have the whole of Irish literature at his disposal. Before about 1770 very few Irish-language documents dealing with Ireland itself had been printed, and most of the language's unprinted writings were inaccessible in private collections. Of the Anglo-Irish cartographers known to history before that time there are probably not more than one or two who ever saw as much as a single page of Irish script. We must remember that in any case the main functions of the written Irish language until the present century were literary, religious, legal and intellectual rather than administrative or managerial. What a cartographer would have wanted was, if not a native map to copy, then at least a native list or table, and that is just what early writers of Irish did not provide.

Our fourth method of name-transmission is by far the most important. The only way I can find to describe it is by the rather misleading word 'dictation'. Of course it was not necessarily the cartographer himself who took the fateful step from speech to writing. It may well have been his source who received the dictation, or perhaps the source of his source, or the source of that source and so on. But as long as the sequence of copying and recopying had begun with

12

a non-Celtic monoglot recording what he heard, then the name at the end of the chain, the name on the map, can count as a dictated name.

How can such names be recognised? One test we have already encountered. It is the absence of spelling habits peculiar to the original language. Consider for instance a Welsh example which happens to point in the opposite direction from the double 'l' I mentioned earlier. In words like 'Mynedd' Saxton and Speed repeatedly substitute 'th' for the correct terminal 'dd', because in such words an Englishman hears the Welshman's 'dd' as 'th'. Another pointer towards dictation is orthographic variability among different scribes attempting to record the same sound. Of course this variability is predictable enough in a language where 'o' can be written as either 'o', 'oh', 'ow', 'owe', 'oe', 'ough', or 'ew'. Also, what the scribe writes is not necessarily what he hears, let alone what he ought to hear. Inaccurate speech or inaccurate listening can make vowels broader or narrower, and change voiced into unvoiced consonants or vice versa. In extreme cases they can eliminate entire syllables. At the same time original sounds absent from the copyist's own language may be replaced by more familiar sounds that resemble them only approximately, as when the sound represented in Irish by 'bh' or dotted 'b' is heard and written by Englishmen as either 'v' or 'f'.

One bizarre and admittedly uncouth feature of this adaptive process is sometimes called assimilation. This involves the use not just of English letter-sequences but of complete English words that partially match the sounds of Irish name-elements while carrying entirely different connotations. We have already met the examples of 'money' and 'beg'. Others are batter (*bothar*, road), boy (*buidhe*, yellow), carrick (*carraig*, rock), drum (*druim*, ridge), glass (*glas*, green), inch (*inis*, island), kill (*cell*, church), knock (*cnoc*, hill), letter (*leitir*, slope), more (*mor*, great), muck (*muc*, pig), roe (*ruadh*, red), ton (*toin*, back), Anna (*eanach*, marsh), Garry (*garrdha*, garden), Owen (*abhainn*, river), Ross (*ros*, wood), Terry (*tir*, land) and Tom (*tuaim*, mound). Here Londoners may be reminded of how 'Infanta of Castile' was corrupted into 'Elephant and Castle', but in these pseudo-Celtic forms there is no such element of false etymology. Despite the violence that haunts Irish history, no-one has ever understood the name 'Kilkenny' as an invitation to homicide. In fact the function of such non-words as 'money', 'beg' etc. is purely conventional: they are simply aids to pronunciation based on the idea of 'look-and-say'. They also serve a mnemonic or labour-saving purpose by standardising elements common to a large number of names. Like translations, they are gestures of respect. The translator respects the sense, the recipient of dictation respects the sound.

In the dictation process as just described we may fairly speak of Irish names as being anglicised. But some recent writers have gone astray in treating anglicisation and translation as alternative strategies that present themselves on the same level of consciousness. At this point we may refer to two particular maps of Ireland, by Jodocus Hondius in 1591 and by Baptista Boazio in 1599. Both include miniature dictionaries of placename elements, perhaps the first of their kind to be found on maps of the British Isles.

J.HONDIUS, 1591: Nomina haec quae passim reperiuntur, ita Anglice intellige. Hybernice/Anglice: Can/Head lant; Enie/lland; Knok/hyll, Rok; C.Carick/Castel; B.Bali/Towne; L.Logh/Lake; Kil/Parishe, town; Slagho/Montains; Glin, Can/Valley; Bog/Bog morish.

B.BOAZIO, 1599: An interpretation in English of some proper Irish names contained in this description of Irelande for the better understanding of the readers. Glyn/a woode; Can/a Promontorie or hed Land; Carick/a rock; Knock/a hill; Slew/a Mountaine; B. or Bale/a Smale towne; Kill/a Village or Parishe towne; Lough/a Lake or great Poole; Enis/ an llande; Mo/a Monasterie.

OS Surveyors Catenary Taping in a Lake, early 20th Century. (Courtesy of OSNI)

Each table has two columns, one for what we would perceive as uncouth anglicised forms such as 'knock' and the other for translated forms such as 'hill' which are English in every sense. The relevance of these tables to the concept of anglicisation is that neither Hondius nor Boazio makes any use of this concept. What we would describe as 'anglicised' they both called simply 'Irish'. Having no idea what real Irish looked like, they assumed that 'kill' and 'knock' actually were Irish. They didn't know they were anglicising, whereas they did of course know that they were translating.

Until the eighteenth century, dictation seems to have been the main source of nomenclature for all cartographers in Ireland who did not simply get their names by copying other maps. This was certainly true of William Petty, at least according to Yann Goblet, the leading expert on him; and it seems also to have been true of Petty's most influential predecessor in Ireland, the Elizabethan surveyor Robert Lythe.

Now, almost by way of parenthesis, our fifth heading, restoration, takes us briefly away from practical expediency into the world of linguistic scholarship, where placename usage became polarised between the ideas of empirical and theoretical, realistic and idealistic, corrupt and pure, modern and ancient. The balance of these opposing forces was not always what might have been predicted. Some Celtic revivalists were themselves wholly non-Celtic in upbringing, birth and descent; while the more cynical realists included not just professional cartographers such as Aaron Arrowsmith, but several eminent and patriotic Celtic scholars like Edward Lhuyd in seventeenth-century Wales and John O'Donovan in nineteenth-century Ireland. Anyway, the number of Celtic forms actually restored by cartographers before the advent of the Ordnance Survey was minute. In mid-eighteenth-century Wales, Lewis Morris deplored the 'murdering' of native names by English mapmakers but did nothing about it. His son William promised a map that would retain the 'British or Celtic' names. He did nothing about it either. In the 1780s and 1790s the Irish language attracted a modicum of sympathy from two otherwise influential Anglo-Irish cartographers, Charles Vallancey and Daniel Beaufort. Between them they restored an Irish-language spelling to a grand total of three placename elements – in two cases incorrectly: Vallancey's was 'cnoc' (a hill), Beaufort's 'Awin' (*Abhainn*, a river) and 'Sliebh' (*Sliabh*, a mountain). No other non-thematic cartographer seems to have made any progress in the same direction, and even in the three instances I have just mentioned most early nineteenth-century maps reverted to the anglicised forms.

These early attempts at restoration may well seem hardly worth mentioning. But there is one less ambitious achievement that deserves notice under the same heading, and that is another kind of standardisation – not now for sound as previously discussed, but for sense. It can be illustrated by three spellings common on pre-nineteenth-century maps, 'drum', 'drom' and 'drim'. All three forms derive from the Irish word for ridge, *druim*, though none of the three is either orthographically or phonetically correct. Instead of trying to revive the Irish version with its uncongenial pairing of 'u' and 'i', a conscientious English cartographer could at least bring out the identity of meaning among the 'drums', 'droms' and 'drims' by choosing one of those three anglicised forms and abandoning both the others. By this expedient, words in that uncouth limbo between Irish and English could assume the character if not of a true language then at any rate of a true vocabulary. Whatever its merits, this idea was at least as old as Hondius and Boazio. In almost every case their tables represented each connotation – 'hill', 'town', 'lake' and the rest – by one and only one spelling. And contemporary cartographers sometimes actually tried to follow the same rule, despite the prevailing climate of orthographic variability. For instance by the 1560s the Irish word for lake, namely 'loch', was already appearing on nearly all maps of Ireland in a single Anglo-Irish form 'lough'.

By the late seventeenth century the processes of substitution, translation, transcription and dictation were all well advanced and most of the Irish geographical names known today had already been subjected to one or other of them. And so experimentation started merging into consolidation. The history of Irish placenames was by no means over, but in the eighteenth century it ran almost exactly parallel with that of English names, and indeed of English words in general, as the ideal of correctness strengthened its grip in the age of Dr. Samuel Johnson. Now it was not just elements common to many names that had to be spelt consistently, but the whole of every individual name.

The more often a name was committed to writing, the sooner it reached its final form. Poverty and illiteracy would clearly be obstacles to standardisation. Its progress could also be influenced by demographic factors. The sparser a population, the less often will its local names be written down. Similarly, small settlements will be named less often in writing than large ones, and most Celtic settlements were small. Thus in Ireland rural population was not generally concentrated into villages but dispersed among the territorial divisions known as townlands, there being on average about twenty-five townlands in each parish. For all these reasons standardisation was slower in the Celtic world than in England. By the eighteenth century this difference was being noticed by

British cartographers. George Taylor and Andrew Skinner in their *Roads of Ireland* (1778), for instance, made a point of apologising for their placenames and of emphasising how hard it had been to collect them. Nevertheless, by the 1800s the range of variation had narrowed considerably. There were now many anglicised spellings of Celtic names that had come to look wrong (even if they sounded no worse than any others), compared with a small and diminishing number that looked right. And I mean looked wrong, or right, to almost everyone. The only people who would dislike the look of all anglicised names were people who could read Irish without being able to read English. How many such people were left in the early nineteenth century? A few thousand? A few hundred?

With the early nineteenth century we finally reach the Ordnance Survey. Under its tutelage, placename cartography in different parts of the British Isles began to diverge. This was mainly because the rise of modern cultural nationalism took place after the large-scale mapping of Ireland by the Ordnance Survey but before the Survey's large-scale mapping of Wales and Scotland. A good deal has been written about Ordnance Survey name policies in Britain so I shall save time by continuing to focus on Ireland. Here the chief purpose of this lecture is to emphasise the continuity between the Survey and its predecessors, and I have deliberately spent a long time making the very simple point that such predecessors did exist. The great majority of the Ordnance Survey's Irish names had already appeared in writing, most of them in writing on maps. So the department could and did choose from written rather than from spoken forms, and in practice the written forms were still necessarily drawn from English-language documents. The Survey also showed considerable respect for spellings that looked right to a majority of its readers. And it continued the long-established policy of standardising recurrent prefixes and suffixes. There was nothing new about any of this. It was exactly what most other cartographers in Ireland had been doing for centuries.

However, the Ordnance Survey did combine these time-honoured practices with one original idea that has not always been properly understood. This was to print not the most common spelling of each name, or the supposed original Irish-language spelling, but whichever of the existing versions was considered to come closest to the original written Irish form, which meant of course that the original Irish form might have to be reconstructed. Having said that, I must add two immediate provisos. One is that this pro-Irish policy was often overridden by other considerations. The other is that 'closest to the original form' did not necessarily mean close in any absolute sense. Consider for example the name 'Ballybeg'. Many Irish townlands bear this name. Suppose we take fifteen of these townlands at random and look them up in the original six-inch Ordnance Survey field name books of the 1830s and 1840s. Altogether the fifteen townlands yield eighty-five earlier written occurrences of the name in question. Not one of these occurrences used the presumed original Irish spelling 'Baile Beag'. In sixty-six cases the spelling was 'Ballybeg', a majority opinion which the Ordnance Survey not unreasonably chose to follow. After centuries of anglicisation, 'Ballybeg' – though it differs from real Irish at five points – was as close to the Irish language as the available written authorities could get. Improbable though this may seem, its choice was governed by a spirit of deference towards the Irish language.

This well-intended break with precedent on the part of the Ordnance Survey has been totally ignored by those authors who accuse the department of leading the trend to anglicisation. These authors are wrong on two counts. First they are wrong about the Survey's priority, as should be clear from what I have already said. Secondly (and this is another point that has come up before) they are wrong on the question of leadership. In its search for historical authenticity the Ordnance Survey revived a number of relatively unfamiliar spellings. But almost the only people in Ireland who followed suit were members of the teaching profession and some, but by no means all, government departments. Other name-users kept faith with the most popular pre-Ordnance Survey spellings, as you can see to this day from innumerable Irish signposts, notice-boards, newspapers, guidebooks and directories, many of them emanating from official sources.

A moment ago I spoke of accusations against the Ordnance Survey. Just who are its accusers? One I have mentioned already is the Irish author Brian Friel, whose play *Translations* has done more than anything else to make the cartography of Celtic names a fashionable subject. *Translations* purports to show the Ordnance Survey in 1833 at Ballybeg, Co. Donegal, choosing the names for a new six-inch map. It is undoubtedly the most beautiful and moving account of the Ordnance Survey ever written, but unfortunately I don't have time to say more about how good it is. Only about how bad it is. I mean how historically bad. Because (as Richard Oliver made clear in a lecture on the Ordnance Survey earlier in the present series), the Survey was not the 'military operation' that this play makes it out to have been. To correct just a few of Friel's mistakes: Ordnance Survey employees were not armed. They did not double as police officers, bailiffs, militiamen, magistrates, or members of the gestapo. They were not empowered to summon private citizens 'for questioning', to level houses, to shoot livestock, or to evict farmers. Their so-called toponymic department was not staffed by the stupidest officers in the British army, or indeed by army officers of any description, but by intelligent civilians familiar with the Irish language.

Why should Brian Friel get the Ordnance Survey's placenames right when he gets everything else wrong? The answer is that he doesn't get them right. One characteristic fallacy is that the Survey was careless and indifferent in its choice of names, a charge easily disproved by looking at one of its field name books. A more specific error is that it was the Ordnance Survey that first put Donegal placenames on the map. In fact the county had already been mapped independently on various scales perhaps fifteen or twenty times. Friel also describes the Survey's task as 'taking' Gaelic names and 'changing them into their approximate English sounds' whereas what the Survey 'took' were not generally Gaelic names but names that other people had already anglicised. A fourth fallacy is that as an alternative to anglicisation the Survey translated names from Irish into English. In Friel's fictitious Ballybeg the department's fictitious translations outnumber its fictitious anglicisations in a ratio of eight to five, the choice between the two processes being fictitiously governed by nothing but pure caprice. In fact it was never the Survey's policy to adopt new translations into English. Of all Friel's untruths the most glaring is the one embodied in his title.

Now you may think that all this is naively to misunderstand a professed work of fiction, and that works of fiction convey not the crude truths of a reference-book but a higher truth of symbols, parables and allegories, their so-called errors being actually no more than various legitimate forms of dramatic licence. That may be what you think but it's not what Brian Friel thinks, as is clear from comments he has made off-stage. For instance when he described Ireland as having been 'rechristened' by the Ordnance Survey he was not writing his play but telling readers of the *Guardian* newspaper what he believed to be authentic Irish history.

So these are not literary devices but real misapprehensions, and they have grown more real through being widely shared. Some writers have independently made the same mistakes as Brian Friel. Thus a professor of geography tells how the Ordnance Survey treated the Irish language as 'an obstacle to be overcome.'[2] This is the exact opposite of the truth for, as we have seen, the Irish language actually provided indispensable assistance in choosing from contradictory authorities. Again, a well-known freelance cartographer anticipates Friel's idea of the Ordnance Survey starting with Gaelic names;[3] and a reviewer in an academic journal quotes the name 'Roundstone' in Co. Donegal as an Ordnance Survey invention when in fact it had been recorded by William Petty as early as 1685.[4]

These more or less innocent errors have mostly arisen from a misunderstanding of the Survey's published maps. But what can we say of errors deriving not from the maps, or from the Survey's non-cartographic records, or from other contemporary writings, or from modern scholarly research, but simply from a single evening in the theatre? Thus a recent book on maps of Scotland prints a real reminiscence of real Ordnance Survey placenames-research in the real Western Isles followed immediately and without comment by a tissue of falsehood from *Translations*.[5] In a recent transatlantic comparison of placename experience, the American evidence is rigorously factual and well-documented while the only Irish source cited is Brian Friel. Admittedly the reader is softened up for the comparison by a clause distinguishing fiction from history, but this disclaimer is quickly forgotten when we slip into phrases like 'these events in Ireland' and 'the destructiveness of alien cartography whether in Ireland or America', as if the terms of the comparison have been established by equally valid methods.[6]

On another occasion, map historians at an international conference were advised by an eminent scholar to see *Translations* if they wanted to know what the Ordnance Survey of Ireland was 'all about'. Elsewhere, Brian Friel has been described as illustrating 'the drama enacted when Ordnance Survey officers struggled with the placenames of Ireland.'[7] Since it is clear from my own postbag that these are not isolated examples, let me state the truth as simply as possible. No drama was enacted when the names of Co. Donegal were mapped in 1833. That was real life. And no Ordnance Survey officers were present in 1980 when *Translations* was performed on stage. They were actors, and their behaviour a baseless fabric, an insubstantial pageant – a play.

None of the writers I have quoted would ever ask the Public Record Office to produce the maps referred to in *King Lear* or *Henry IV*. Why make such a muddle of fact and fiction in this case? There are various not very creditable answers to that question. To save time, let's just say that Ireland has worked its spell, and finish instead with a more general comment. Map history is a subject in which two strands have recently become distinguishable. We might call them the professional and the ideological. On the one hand, cartographic scholars have addressed the outside world from within the circle of their expertise. This, they say, is how maps were made; or, if you like, how mapmakers differed from the rest of us. Meanwhile, from outside the circle, philosophers, sociologists, semiologists and others have been harvesting a larger wisdom. These, they say, are the universal truths that maps exemplify, this is how their authors resemble the rest of us.

Ideological map history has given its readers a thought-provoking and entertaining experience, which I never thought did anyone very much harm until I saw fiction being openly preferred to history in a case that I happened to be familiar with. But in Ireland theories – of imperialism or racism or whatever – have been generating what purport to be factual statements about real people and real maps. 'Here are cartographers acting for an alien government', runs the Brian Friel scenario. 'They must have robbed a native population of its names'. Except that they didn't. A small tract of scholar's territory has been invaded by the forces of political correctness and needs to be reclaimed.

Notes

1.   This paper is an edited version of a lecture given at the Warburg Institute, London, in May 1992 as part of a series on 'Maps and Society' organised by Catherine Delano Smith (Queen Mary and Westfield College) and Tony Campbell (Map Library, British Library).

2.   Jones Hughes, T., review of L.M. Cullen, *The emergence of modern Ireland* in *Irish Geography*, xv (1982), pp. 131-3.

3.   Robinson, T.D., 'Aran surrounded by water', *Geographical Magazine*, xlix (1976), p. 178.

4.   Bradbeer, John, review of Tim Robinson, *Connemara* in *Cartographic Journal*, xxviii (1991), p. 134.

5.   Macleod, Finlay (ed.), *Togail tir, marking time: the map of the Western Isles* (Stornoway, 1989), pp. 97-112 and preface.

6.   Harley, J.B., 'What happens when we've made a map', lecture, Penn State University, 1991, pp. 6-8, 11, 16; Harley, J.B., 'Victims of a map: New England cartography and the native Americans', typescript, September 1990, pp. 10-11, 16.

7.   Wallis, Helen, review of Finlay Macleod (ed.), *Togail tir* in *Journal of the International Map Collectors' Society*, xliv (1991), p. 37.

The Letters of John O'Donovan in County Fermanagh : Dogs, Turkeycocks and Ganders

J.B. Cunningham

John O'Donovan was born in the townland of Attateemore in County Kilkenny on 9th July in 1809 and is probably the most celebrated Irish scholar ever. He is owed an immense debt of gratitude by us all for the range, accuracy and extent of his studies.

He was educated in Dublin and worked in the Irish Record Office before joining the Ordnance Survey in 1829 at the age of twenty. His work with the Survey took him to every parish in Ireland and there he recorded and investigated local manuscripts as well as the spellings, derivations and authenticity of the huge numbers of placenames which were then being engraved on to the Ordnance Survey maps of Ireland. He constantly recorded his observations on these matters in letters back to Dublin and long afterwards these were edited by Fr. Michael O'Flanagan and are of such an enormous bulk that it required fifty volumes to publish them. This was the first of many scholarly works undertaken by O'Donovan and many of these were published by the Irish Archaeological Society which he and Eugene O'Curry founded in 1840. Among the subjects he wrote about were poetry, history, law, topography and genealogy and invariably he included old maps and translations of the ancient Irish Texts. His greatest work was his edition and translation of the Annals of the Four Masters in seven volumes between 1848 and 1851. He published a grammar of the Irish Language in 1845 and transcribed and translated nine volumes of the ancient Irish legal manuscripts which he unfortunately did not live to edit. He died in Dublin on the 9th of December 1861 at the age of 52.

The letters which he wrote in County Fermanagh tell of the information he collected in the county during the progress of the Ordnance Survey and in telling us what he found he also tells us a great deal about himself and the county of Fermanagh in the early part of the last century. His first letter of twenty-six letters concerning Fermanagh was sent to his superiors in Dublin on Friday evening, October 10th, 1834. He has just arrived in Enniskillen.

In it he recounts that he had great difficulty in getting to County Fermanagh at all and he goes on to tell of his trials and tribulations. He was on his way to

Fermanagh from Maghera, and on the first leg of this journey as far as Derry he only just managed to get an outside seat on the coach on a terribly wet and stormy October day. There was a gathering of clergymen in Derry that day and as a result space on the coach was at a premium. Now he does not say that all of the clergymen were safe and secure inside the coach but perhaps just gives us that impression. On their way through the Glenshane Pass those on the outside of the coach were drenched to the skin by wind-driven showers and the conditions were so bad that their very umbrellas were torn into ribbons. I do not know what was going through the heads of the rest of the passengers on the coach, but perhaps some were wondering, Would the bishop be in a foul mood? Has some parishioner complained about me? How soon is the next toilet stop? or perhaps, simply, how soon can I get a stiff drink? But not John O'Donovan. As a true historian he sat there with the water running off the ruins of his umbrella, down on to his thighs and legs and eventually even out of his shoes and he reflected, as indeed would all committed historians have reflected; that is in a historical manner. He surveyed the bleak landscape and the terrible day and drawing on his historical knowledge concluded that the ancients had the right idea when they called this place, the Glenshane Pass, *An Gleann Sion* – the valley of storms.

In just this little section of one of his letters we learn a lot about the man, John O'Donovan, for he was one who constantly saw the world about him in historical terms as he looked around. Looking out over any particular landscape he saw not the fields and groves of his day but instead the territories of ancient tribes, the sites of battlefields of long ago and the general historical backdrop against which the great events occurred which were chronicled in the volumes of the old Irish Annals. Perhaps all historians do the same to some extent and therefore do not see it as strange or unusual that John O'Donovan did not swear at the coachman or think about a drink but rather endured the ghastly conditions and thought historical thoughts. All historians can identify with him.

But this is only the beginnings of his difficulties in getting to County Fermanagh and as he recounts them in his letter we can also better understand what travellers in this part of the world had to endure in the early part of the last century. Having reached Derry he engaged a seat on the coach named "The Fair Trader" bound for Enniskillen with ten passengers inside and eighteen passengers outside. Needless to say John O'Donovan was one of the unlucky ones on the outside and the coach set off at four in the afternoon heading into a strong wind, again, accompanied by rain. It was carrying a company of noisy, drunken passengers. It seems that being well inebriated was one of the preferred states in which to travel in those days and especially so when it was cold and wet. By the time he got to Strabane his feet were so numb with cold that he prepared to alight to get a stiff glass of whiskey to help restore his circulation. Some of the passengers were staying overnight in Strabane and as they alighted fighting broke out among those struggling to take their places. Suddenly, realising what was going to happen O'Donovan turned back to hold on to his seat but found that it was gone. Nothing bar physical force would get it back.

And so there he was stranded in no man's land without a drink to revive himself and unable to eject the pugnacious holder of his seat. In the end, simply in order to continue his journey, he is forced to occupy the most precarious seat on top of a trunk at the highest point of the coach.

He tries to make the best of his situation, as he puts it, halfway between heaven and earth and surrounded by noisy, drunken, fellow passengers. Suddenly, so numb with cold that he did not know whether he was killed or not, he found himself lying in a field quite a way from the coach asking himself the following questions. As he records in his letter, the questions were: Am I killed? Am I crippled? Are my brains dashed out? In the end, when he finally collected his thoughts, and got to his feet he found that the driver had carelessly or drunkenly allowed the right wheel of the coach into the drain. All the outside passengers had been hurled off the coach and he being the highest up shot through the air the furthest. He was thankful that he did not sustain worse than a severe bruising of his left side and arm and the coach was righted by the combined strength of the passengers and away they went and finished their journey to Omagh where he stayed the night.

He arose early the next morning about half past five and arrived at the coach office in Omagh, as he believed, in plenty of time, to get the coach to Enniskillen. To his amazement and intense anger he found that the coach had gone. It had simply departed early because there was an unusually large crowd going to Enniskillen Fair Day and even though he had booked and paid for his seat the coach had gone without him. He was livid. In fact he was so livid that he set out to walk from Omagh to Enniskillen and such were the roads of the day that he arrived there only a few hours after the coach on which he should have travelled. Moreover he says that he wasn't in the least fatigued by the effort as his vexation and anger had carried him along without feeling tired.

However, he spent the next day indoors as he had developed a cold and busied himself in getting his papers in order and reading up the Fermanagh related extracts from the Annals of Ulster which had been sent to him. These he would be constantly referring to on his travels around the county.

He was apparently expected to get through his work in Fermanagh in a month but informed his superiors in this letter that this period would never be long enough as the county was far too interesting and there was so much to be seen. His next letter is dated October 12th, 1834 and is again from Enniskillen.

He had spent his day in his new lodgings hard at work indexing the references to County Fermanagh that he had been sent but found them to be lacking. As a result his next letter lists 24 placenames in Fermanagh that he wishes to have looked up in the Annals and all references to them sent on to him immediately. His enquiries are in particular for entries for the various Baronies of Fermanagh such as Lurg and Magherastephena. He also wants entries relating to islands in Lough Erne and to the names of individual places and villages such as Belleek, Kinawley and Killesher. He also wants all references sent to him about notable Fermanagh families like Maguire and O'Cassidy.

He writes again on October 15th 1834 from Enniskillen and tells of his first major disappointment in the County. As the Maguires had been the most notable of Fermanagh Families, O'Donovan was keen to meet the current representative of the ancient line. He found that, Thomas Maguire, the descendant of the last Lord of Enniskillen was a hardware merchant in Enniskillen and worse still than his occupation, as far as O'Donovan was concerned, was that he was a man with little or no regard for the fact that he was, as it were, of Irish Royal Blood.

O'Donovan remarks that he found him like all shopkeepers totally devoid of patriotic feelings. (I suppose if O'Donovan ever had to run a shop for a living he might feel the same way himself.) Despite the fact that he was even pointed out by Lord Enniskillen as **The Maguire**, Thomas humbly plied his trade in knives and forks, spoons, combs, buckles, hinges and bridles apparently oblivious to the heritage he represented. O'Donovan thought this to be a terrible "come down" from the ancient majesty of the Maguires and insult was added to injury by Thomas Maguire's total lack of interest or appreciation of his ancestry. In dismissing the disappointing figure of Thomas Maguire, O'Donovan remarks that he would prefer the barefooted Bryan Mann Mullan, who lived in a little cabin in the wilds of Glenuller and although he possessed nothing of the goods of this world yet retained an awareness and appreciation of his forefathers and the ancient heritage which he happened to represent.

In the same letter he takes Lord Enniskillen to task for his promotion of the idea that Enniskillen's name was derived from the finding of a shilling on a little island near the East Bridge or from that island's resemblance to a shilling coin. He derides this idea as the sort of pedantic story which he continually ran across in his work whereby foolish old men who don't know why a place has got its name proceed to invent an explanation loosely based on the sound of the word. They do this, he says, rather than plainly admit as to their entire ignorance in the matter. He asserts that the island or Innis took its name from Ceithleanna, a man's name in Pagan times, indeed a name long pre-dating any shilling coin whatever and that the town gets it's name as the Island of Ceithleanna.

He notes in the same letter a canine attack on his colleague, Mr. Downes, and he hopes that the dog that attacked Downes has been shot. He says that he has been frequently attacked by regiments of dogs but has been fortunate in his escape so far. He adds that the attacks have not been confined to dogs along but that also he has been attacked by turkey cocks and ganders.

In his work new topographical words are of great interest to him and he notes in his letter that the word Tate is common in Fermanagh and although the Parish Priest of Enniskillen assures him that this word is the same as the word Bally he has a well founded notion in his head that this word Tate denotes an ancient measure of land.

The frequency of O'Donovan's letters is remarkable and on the day following the last letter, October 16th 1834 he writes again from Enniskillen to remark that townlands with O,Ua or Mac he is certain denote townlands linked to a family name as in Ballymacelroy or Ballymacsherry. Others such as old Alick Ogilby are determined that all townland names should describe the locality but he is as certain in his belief as they are in theirs.

In the same letter in discussing the employment of a Mr. Curry in the Ordnance Service he gives a revealing insight into the conditions under which he himself works. He notes that his job is not well paid and that surprisingly he could live more comfortably in Dublin on a pound a week than out in the country for three pounds a week. One of the hazards of his job apparently is that in every inn he establishes himself and acquires a reputation as an honest, quiet fellow he gets hounded from the premises by females looking for money to provide public entertainment in the place. He then has to shift his quarters and, as he says, "dine on rusty bacon and sour beer and sleep in damp beds and get charged top rates for inferior service and conditions."

In dismissing Mr. Curry as unsuitable for the position at least in the northern half of Ireland he strikes a peculiarly discordant note when he says that Curry, who is based in Limerick, would be unable at present to deal with the northern pronunciation and would remain unable to do so until he was better acquainted with the "Northern peculiarities and barbarisms." Perhaps he more sensitively defines the role of those like himself employed by the Ordnance Survey in the letter when he says:

"No person is fit or should be allowed to meddle with those names except one acquainted with the whole circle of Irish lore and with the peculiarities of pronunciation that prevail in the different districts."

He continues to stay in Enniskillen and writes from there on Friday 17th October 1834.

The town of Enniskillen which is now in the Barony of Tirkennedy, he believes, was once in the Barony of Cuil, C U I L or as it is now styled Coole. The local Irish refer to Castle Coole as Caislean Na Cuile and the Maguires and O'Cassidys were addressed as Maguidir Na Cuile, i.e. Maguire of the Coole or O'Cassidy of the Coole.

O'Donovan has recently met a Captain Gabbot in Enniskillen, a magistrate and a man who amazed him with his knowledge of the general topography and history of Ireland. On the other hand he was able to astonish Captain Gabbot with details from the Irish Annals as the Captain did not know that there existed such ancient records in the Irish language. This letter contains a long genealogical passage concerning the Maguires of Fermanagh. He traces their line of descent according to a manuscript supplied to him by Mr. O'Reilly. In addition, he gives a genealogy of the McManus's, a branch of the Maguire family and that of another notable Fermanagh family, the McGaffreys or McCaffreys. He lists other noteworthy Fermanagh families as the MacElroys, the MacBriens, the O'Breslins, the O'Corcrans, the O'Cadhans, the O'Corracains, the O'Mochans, the Muldoons and many others.

He writes again from Enniskillen on Monday, 20th October 1834 and he requests more information on the Barony of Clonkelly, on the village of Tempo and on Sgiath Gabhra where the chiefs of Fermanagh were inaugurated. He reports that the weather is stormy and wet, the days short and the roads heavy and water-logged. Fermanagh he notes is much more stormy and wet than Derry or Down.

The Fermanagh Irish, that is the Irish language spoken in Fermanagh, he finds to be very like that of Connaught and the townland names are very

27

different to those of the other Ulster counties. New topographical words are occurring in every parish.– Tates, Goba, Rosses and Rings occur frequently.

He visits one of Fermanagh's greatest antiquities on 21st October, viz Devenish Island and writes from there on the following day. The island's most famous structure, the round tower, which was perfect there four months ago is lamentably injured through storm damage and if not soon repaired will loose it's conical top. The jackdaws have carried seeds to the damaged area and the resulting seedling trees, principally alder, have loosened the stones. It pains him to see beautifully hewn stones, ornamented with heads crashing down and smashing against each other. Lord Enniskillen and Lord Ely have both offered to pay for the work but everyone is afraid of the height. Captain Bentham of the 53rd Regiment is apparently very keen to have it repaired and he has the command of enough men to do the job but is reluctant to do it lest they make a botch of it.

The Barony of Lurg, in western Fermanagh, he says is looked upon by the rest of Fermanagh as different to all the others. The people there differ from the rest in customs and manners and in a great degree in dialect. The "Men of Lurg" he notes is as common an expression today as "Feara Luirg" was six hundred years ago and with good reason as he later explains.

Moving away from Enniskillen, O'Donovan firstly travels west to Derrygonnelly from where he writes on 22nd October. He now believes that Fermanagh should be called the Land of Storms or Patria Ventorum since he has never experienced such storms as toss the waters of Lough Erne. He had walked to Derrygonnelly through wind and rain an estimated eight miles. He was wet through by the first quarter of an hour and with all the water he was carrying thought that he must have weighed fourteen stone. He looked so black as the result of the stream of black water flowing from his hat down his back and face that he could hardly get a place to stay in Derrygonnelly. Still he reports that he enjoyed the sight of the wind driven clouds and the different varieties of rain he experienced, from torrential downpours to misty drops swept along by the wind. On the next day the weather was still so bad that he did not venture out in it. He remarks that he is now in the lands of the ancient Irish family of O'Flannigans, who, although formerly respectable i.e. Irish Nobility, were now all dwindled to petty farmers, cottiers and public house keepers. (Almost all of the ancient Irish he comes in contact with are seemingly a disappointment to John O'Donovan.) He continues to stay in the same village of Derrygonnelly and again writes from there on the 25th October 1834.

28

He wants Dublin to urgently send him all information on the escape of Red Hugh O'Donnell from Dublin in 1587 and his final section of the journey through Fermanagh. He is seeking information too about Kiltierney Church, near Kesh, which was set on fire on one St. Patrick's Day by the men of one branch of the Maguires while his rival was inside at Mass. He also mentions the plundering of various islands on Lough Melvin. He particularly wants all references in the Annals to the fords over the River Erne at the Narrow Water or Cael Uisge at the lower end of Lough Erne in which direction he is now heading.

Having moved further to the west he writes from Castle Caldwell, near Belleek, on 30th October 1834. There he remarks of the great flag or flat stone in the river Erne at Belleek from which Belleek, Beal Leice, gets it's name. This flagstone was as level as a floor and invariably dry and above the water in the summer; now in winter, when O'Donovan sees it, it was entirely under water. He also mentions Stony Island or Still-house Island near Garrison. It's alternative name of Still-house Island coming from the practice of poiteen making which was apparently fairly openly carried on there. At Castle Caldwell, to his delight, he found a museum and was much interested in it. There were many exotic items in the museum which had been founded by Sir John Caldwell, the last of the Caldwells and who had recently died. O'Donovan, however, only really cared for the items of Irish interest and chief among these was the skull of the celebrated Irish musician, O'Carolan.

Major Bloomfield who had married one of the daughters of Sir John Caldwell was now in charge of the Castle Caldwell museum but had little interest in it. The Major was willing to give O'Donovan the skull of the celebrated musician but he was not able to take it with him at the time, not having a suitable box in which to carry this rather gruesome relic of the past.

From Kesh on 31st October 1834, O'Donovan reports on his recent stay at Castle Caldwell where he had spent two days. He found the castle to be too fashionable a gentleman's house for such a hardworking man as himself. There was too much time spent on wining and dining and he was impatient to get on with his work. He thought the Castle museum was a splendid one. Old Sir John Caldwell had lavished great attention on it. Along with its collection of stuffed exotic birds and animals were American Indian weapons and dress which he had personally obtained while living with the Objibwa Indians and these stood side by side with exotic implements such as a negro beheading axe. As a collection it was in many ways a simple testament to the travels and history of the Caldwell family over centuries.

However while O'Donovan admired the unusual and bizzarre in the Caldwell collection he was really only interested in the Irish items there. Things like kegs of preserved butter found in the bog, the ancient lock of Donegal Castle, the harp of O'Neill, another famous musician, a gun from the Spanish Armada, bronze cauldrons and containers, stone and bronze axes, a fragment of Irish chain mail and some ancient Irish ecclesiastical bells attributed to local saints were the items he particularly noted.

However it was O'Carolan's skull that fascinated him most of all and he records his reading of the skull in accordance with the, then, fashionable doctrines of Dr. Spurgheim who believed that the character of a person could be deduced from the ridges, indentations and bumps on it's surface. In addition to this analysis of the skull, O'Donovan reports the existence of a small hole bored over the right eye of the skull by the brother of Lord Roscommon through which a ribbon had been tied, presumably as a decoration. (Personally, I wonder did they ever think that O'Carolan might have preferred to have his skull properly and decently buried and not be decorated with ribbons or perhaps it really should be desecrated with ribbons.)

The extreme west of Fermanagh and particularly the narrow part of the Erne from the lower lake to the sea features so often in the Annals as Cael Uisge or the Narrow Water that O'Donovan is determined to view every crossing place along this ancient and much contested frontier. He walks the banks of the Erne between Belleek and Ballyshannon to view all the old fords recorded in the Annals and also circled the adjacent Plain of Moy Kedne passing from Ballyshannon to Lough Melvin. He is delighted in travelling around this picturesque lake which he describes as one of the most beautiful and romantic in the world but despite its beauty he still describes its banks as desolate and dreary. The reason he gives for saying this was that there was not a gentleman's residence anywhere along its shores. O'Donovan ends this particular letter in a hurry due to the disturbances of Halloween night "in this wild country village" – Kesh. Despite the disturbances he continues to stay there and pens another letter from the same village on 31st October 1834.

He again talks about his stay at Castle Caldwell but says that he decided to move on, since, although Major Bloomfield has been very kind to him he was unable to dine, lunch or take tea and wine after the Major's fashion. However he has been amazingly gratified with his visit there. Major Bloomfield had sent for all the old sheanachies in the neighbourhood and apparently told them that O'Donovan was going to make them all Barons of Toora or of Lurg. Despite the assistance he has received from the Major and all the hospitality bestowed upon him, O'Donovan is unable to warm to his host at Castle Caldwell. His final verdict on him is that "he is a very good upright man but too anti-Irish for me." He ends with the remark that this letter has been written with a very bad pen in a very smoky place in his inn in Kesh.

By 4th November 1834, O'Donovan has circled Lower Lough Erne and is back in Enniskillen. In this letter he comments on the bells on display in the Castle Caldwell museum and suspects that the largest of them is the bell of St. Ninny, a saint very much identified with County Fermanagh. (These bells are at present in the National Museum of Antiquities in Scotland.) He finds that the tower at Devenish is still unrepaired but that a considerable sum of money has been subscribed to have the job done. There is still however the major problem concerning the erection of scaffolding on the round tower. The Enniskillen builders are afraid that if the scaffolding is erected and secured by means of the top windows of the tower the storm would catch it and the whole thing be torn down. Most advise waiting until the spring but then the military officer whose men would do the job is likely to be gone.

He tells Dublin that there is a great report in the area suggesting that Constantine Maguire, the Tempo landlord, has been shot dead in County Tipperary. He had been previously shot and wounded on his estate near Tempo in a land dispute and his assassin, by the name of Rutledge, had been hanged for the attack. This land dispute had arisen when some farmers enclosed part of the mountain land belonging to Constantine near Tempo and he had ordered their hedges destroyed and a new boundary well erected around his property. O'Donovan wants Dublin to send him all details of the incident as soon as possible.

From Enniskillen on the 6th of November 1834 he again notes the influence of Connaught Irish on Fermanagh as being very strong. The termination Reagh he is obliged to make Reevagh and Garrow into Garve to suit Fermanagh pronunciation. Taobh meaning side or brae-face the Ordnance has previously anglicised as Tieve which is proving too violent an innovation in Fermanagh. Most authorities in Fermanagh he finds wish to make it Teev rather than the more northerly Tee-oov. He finds that the land proprietors are frequently very displeased if they find that too big a change has been made in the spelling of a townland but he says he has no wish to be controlled in his judgments by the views of the landowners since he has found in his experience that they know very little about the subject and what they do know is generally wrong or simply pedantic. He finds the word Cashel, meaning an enclosure built of stone

31

to be well understood in Fermanagh although not understood in Derry or any other county that he has been in. *Deanaighidhe caisiol do' n eallach,* "Erect a cashel for the cattle," he found well understood in Toora an area between Derrygonnelly and Belleek.

The Irish word Iubhar meaning a yew tree he also finds frequently in Fermanagh despite the fact that one authority claims that the tree is not native to Ireland. He has found it growing in luxuriance on the cliffs of Fweealt in Toora and elsewhere on cliffs and rock faces in the townland of Monawilkin.

Referring to his visit to the Derrygonnelly area O'Donovan notes that the Irish name for Monea was Muine Fhiadh or the hill of the deer. Apparently St. Faber's pet deer pointed out this site as the place where she might erect her church. The saint had previously tried to erect her church nearby at Kildrum at what had been a sacred well of the ancient pre-Christian beliefs. However anything built at this site during the day was knocked down during the night by some powerful invisible being and in the end the saint was forced to move elsewhere. Obviously the old beliefs remained strong in this area and here the old Gods had no intention of being ousted from their ancient place of worship.

Later this "petted" deer of the St. Faber was crossing the Sillees River in the locality carrying the saint's books on it's antlers and was caused to slip on the muddy banks of the river by the Genii or Spirit of the river, known as Shaver in Irish as in the nearby "Glen a Shaver" meaning the Glen of the Spirit. This spirit continued to resist the encroachment of Christianity in the area and for this act the River Sillees was cursed by the saint that it might be sterile in fish, be destructive in human life and be forced to run uphill. Even an inanimate object apparently does not lightly cross an Irish saint!

All these old tales of spirits and mysterious and magical occurrences fascinate O'Donovan and he records them all. He talks of the stone coffin on Devenish Island of a peculiar shape and apparently anyone able to fit into it is cured of whatever malady they are afflicted. Holy wells are another of these mysterious and miraculous occurrences in the Fermanagh countryside and in the Kinawley area he later notes a holy well that had the power to cure jaundice ever since the handle of the bell of St. Naile was dipped in it. Again he writes later concerning two wells in Fermanagh, one dedicated to St. Molasha, and one dedicated to St. Thady both of whom cure the yellow jaundice. Over in Templecarne Parish he notes the townland of Portnablahy or the "port of the buttermilk" where O'Flanagan landed his butter and his milk which he paid in tribute to O'Donnell. This may well have been handed over at the great market held at Margay Hill near Pettigo.

O'Donovan lists the chief families of the Barony of Lurg as follows:

- The Muldoons—no longer chieftains and no higher ranking than farmers but very decent respectable men, fond of justice and very able in a fight. He records that a dozen of the warlike men of Lurg, **Feara Luirg**, would beat a funeral of the men of any other Barony in the County. They are tall and stout with large heads and round faces.

- The O'Cassidys who originally came from Ballycassidy three miles north of Enniskillen.

- The McGoldricks who were numerous about Belleek.

- The McMulkins; McGraths; Scollans; Gilfedders and Galloglys and the O'Galladas, the guards of Lough Melvin.

The process of Anglicisation of native Irish names O'Donovan deplores greatly and he especially notes this in action as the people come from the rural areas move into Enniskillen. As an example the O'Hones anciently, officials of Lough Erne, are now called Hoynes in the country and once arrived in Enniskillen have transformed their name yet again and become Owens. O'Donovan records an example of this anglicising process in the case of a Mr. J. Owens of Enniskillen who was described to him as being the son of Mr. J. Hoynes of Boho. The O'Leanain another Fermanagh name has been anglicised to Lannon and the name MacGille Finnen first changed to McEllinnion and has now as O'Donovan puts it, been shamefully anglicised to Leonard. MacCosgraigh and MacGilla Coisgle have both become McCuskers and although it is difficult to trace the origin of some of the names O'Donovan finds that the purest records of the ancient names is still kept in the mountains where there they are strictly maintained.

It is always O'Donovan's custom, "to send into the mountains" to get the old men of the area and question them at length in order to arrive at the oldest truths of local history. As he later remarks this type of information does not come cheaply. The old sheanachies need to be entertained and tongues have to be loosened at O'Donovan's expense before they will part with their information. Nothing has obviously changed in this regard!

In his letter of 10th November 1834 he comments on the ancient Barony of Muintir Pheodachain between Lough Ma Nean and Lough Erne. This does not exist any more but Belmore Mountain in this Barony was known as Bel Mor Mhuintir Pheodachain and the area was probably the territory of the McGoverns.

O'Donovan has found out that his beloved Annals of Ulster, which he has been studying so closely were compiled at Belisle to the east of Enniskillen near Lisbellaw and he believes that he is the first man in modern times to have discovered this. What he really means is that he is the first scholar to be aware of this since the old sheanachies of the country knew this all along. It was only the scholars that had lost the information.

As in other areas O'Donovan lists what he calls, "the aboriginal families of Cleenish and Killesher." These are MacScollog now anglicised Farmer, Lunny, Fee, MacEllinnion now anglicised to Leonard, Killesher or Giolla Laisre now Green, Lally or Lilly, O'Hone or Owens, McHughs, MacUltachan, McIlloon, Dolans, Mac a Reevy, MacManus and Coracans who are described as "rattling good fellows fond of fight and fun." MacAuleys are numerous in Clanawley Barony. One of Maguires sons called Amhlaoibh pronounced Amley and MacAuleys are his descendants and were given the Clanawley area to live in.

Many stories, he reports, are now told of Captain Cuhonny Maguire of Tempo. Another tells that when Bryan Maguire and the late Constantine Maguire were children they used to shoot apples off each others heads and that their father, Hugh, delighted in this most peculiar "game".

Before writing from Belturbet on 12th November 1834, O'Donovan had just walked there from Florencecourt keeping Beann Eachlabhra or Benaughlin Mountain for a long time in view. He recounts that Donn Maguire the first Maguire prince of Fermanagh inhabits the mountain and when any of his descendants die a splink is supposed to fall from the rocky face of the cliff on the mountain. He goes by the name of Donn na Binne now in afterlife and presides over all the fairies in Fermanagh. One tradition states that he helped the Maguires in a battle against the English and that when their ammunition was exhausted they gained victory through throwing stones.

He locates the site of the Battle of the Biscuits in the sixteenth century at Drummane Bridge on the Arney River four miles from Enniskillen. The battle got its name from the amount of hard army biscuit left behind by the retreating English.

In Kinawley Parish he met a very intelligent old man called Torlagh or Terrance Carran who was steeped in tradition and legendary lore. He learns from Terrance that in this locality the descendants of the different branches of the Maguires were still being pointed out, e.g. Slioct an Abba, (the breed or descendants of the Abbot), Sliocht Philip na Tuaighe (the breed or descendants of Philip of the Battleaxe). This tradition still continues in parts of Fermanagh today.

From Enniskillen on the 15th November 1834, he writes that he has walked from Belturbet to Enniskillen in four and a half hours a distance of eighteen miles and proves that whatever else he was, O'Donovan was a very fit young man.

From Tempo on Monday, 17th November 1834 he writes to say that he is puzzled by the name of the village of Ballinamallard. The name may arise from Bel Aith na Mallacht meaning the ford of the curses or perhaps, as local legend has it, that it was a place where the Maguires were disappointed in the late arrival of their allies to defend this place as one of the three great passes between Enniskillen and Derry. This second interpretation of the name of Ballinamallard would mean that it derived it's name from Bel Aith na Mall Theacht – the ford of the late arrival. O'Donovan is inclined to accept the former meaning as deriving from some ancient massacre which took place at the ford.

From Tempo on the 18th November, 1834, O'Donovan writes of going into the mountains to get information concerning the townland names and there meets a very intelligent man by the name of Patrick Maguire who owns a great deal of the mountain and is considered a wealthy man.

While in this area he also has visited Tempo Manor which is in a ruined and decayed state. All of this he attributes to Captain Hugh Maguire who took no care to look after the affairs of the family. Some people even believe that there is a curse over these Maguires. Tempo is reputed to have acquired its name as a result of St. Patrick ordering one of his servants to return to where he had been last and fetch the manuscript that he had left behind him, the Irish word *Tiompoidh* meaning to turn. O'Donovan on the other hand considers that the village has got it's name from the remarkable turnings or windings of the Tempo River and tells of two local men in America who fell out and one remarked that the other was as twisted as the Tempo River.

He reflects on the various branches of the Maguire Family today and how they and other ancient Irish Families have declined. In a sweeping generalisation he declares that their downfall has come about through war, women and madness. In an illustration of the latter two of his reasons for genealogical decay among the old Irish aristocracy, he states that Captain Hugh Maguire

35

when an old man turned out his wife, the mother of his nine legitimate children and replaced her with the housemaid. He sees the Maguires, the O'Donovans and the O'Neills all coming to the end of their legitimate male lines and Lord O'Neill is of particular concern. He has no known issue legitimate or illegitimate as a result of foolishly confining his interest in females, solely to other men's wives.

From Newtownbutler on 19th November 1834, he considers the question of restoring the ancient townland name of Ballymacelroy to the map. It has been dropped by the Boundary Surveyor in favour of Mullaghkeel. Since it was the seat of the ancient family of MacGiolla Ruaidh who have been anglicised to MacGilroy, McElroy and Gilroy and are still numerous in the area he would like to see the old name restored. He also mentions the townland of Ballymacaffrey as being the seat of another ancient Fermanagh Clan and again the name is common in the neighbourhood.

He puzzles over three common topographical words in Fermanagh viz Corr, Esh and Tate. As far as he can understand Corr refers to the word odd, Esh to a hill and Tate to a measure of land of approximately sixty acres or one quarter of a townland. The word Tate he has only found in Fermanagh and Tyrone. Some other words which he has only found in Fermanagh as place names are mentioned. The associated words, sreuch and creach refer to a level area on the mountain.

From Maguiresbridge on Saturday, 20th November 1834 O'Donovan refers to the thief's stone, a tall stone in Galloon Parish where a sheep stealer stopped to lean his burden. His booty slipped off the top of the stone and the attached strap slipping up around his throat hanged him.

Having returned to Enniskillen he writes on Monday, November 24th, 1834 that he has found out more about Muintir-Pheodachain and its most ancient chiefs the MacGillionnions who have anglicised their names to Leonard. He had originally thought that the McGovern people had ruled this ancient area.

He goes on to comment on the mountainous area between Garrison and Derrygonnelly known as The Dogs or in Irish, Slieve Da Chon, the Mountain of the Two Dogs. These are supposed to be the two hounds of Finn MacCool who were metamorphised into adjacent hills by a witch who had taken on the shape of a doe. O'Donovan had been told this story of the Two Dogs in Derrygonnelly by a man called Hugh O'Flanagan who had come into the village one night to share with O'Donovan all he knew about the territory of his ancestors, the ancient territory of the O'Flanagans.

Hugh was a man who apparently limited his drinking to two glasses of whisky in the day and after his talk with the man from the Ordnance Survey found himself reluctant to leave Derrygonnelly without taking in his daily allowance. So he stayed in the village until the moon got up before setting off home and unfortunately left behind him in the pub the makings of a pair of shoes. He searched in vain for them the following day and when he couldn't find his belongings claimed the price of the makings of the shoes off O'Donovan or at least he tried to. Hugh failed to get anything from O'Donovan but in this letter he regrets not having given him something and hopes to recompense him in the future. He had tried to assure Hugh O'Flanagan that the information he was giving him was rescuing the family name from oblivion but Hugh was entirely unmoved by this. His ancient family had left him nothing and as far as Hugh was concerned as they had thought nothing of him and he thought nothing of them.

In his letter from Enniskillen on November 24th 1834 O'Donovan announces that he is heading for Dublin on Wednesday morning.

Since he seems to have walked everywhere he incurred no travelling expenses in Fermanagh except two shillings that he paid a fisherman for rowing himself and Lt. Taylor across Lough Melvin. He has spent a long time in the county but he has not been a minute idle, day or night, he says, since he came here. However he does complain that he has been at considerable expense in entertaining the old sheanachies for whom he had sent to the mountains.

He tells the story of Sliabh Beatha, a mountain running twenty-four miles through Fermanagh and Monaghan and the inhabitants style themselves as people of this mountain and welcome strangers to their part of the world with the rhyming words *Se do bheatha air Shliabh Beatha* – You are welcome on Sliabh Beatha.

In another record of the spirit world of County Fermanagh O'Donovan notes that in the huge cairn on this mountain the antedeluvian figure, Bioth, was interred by the seraglio of women who attended him. However, now, apparently this king of the fairies has been replaced by Dalach who is now commander in chief and resides in the Carn More or Great Carn on the top of the mountain. He asserts that Bith or Bioth was a man's name for a long time in Ireland, and the gaelic parts of Scotland, and that Shakespeare has immortalised the name in one of his most famous characters viz McBith or MacBeth. In Ireland the name MacBeatha he says has been anglicised as McVeagh.

With obvious relish O'Donovan recounts, as we would expect him to, a good townland story. This is the story of Luke Cassidy going to pay his rent to Mr. Madden of Spring Grove in the parish of Clones and of Cassidy meeting Lord Erne near his landlord's house. Cassidy did not know Lord Erne and when Lord Erne asked him where he was going Cassidy gave him a smart answer and said he was going to give justice. Quizzed as to how he could be going to give justice and asked whether or not he was a magistrate, Cassidy replied, that he was going to give his landlord his rent and asked was this not giving justice. Lord Erne then wanted to know whether Cassidy would entrust him with the rent and Cassidy replied that he would as long as he gave him a receipt and spelt correctly the townland in which he lived.

Lord Erne got more than he bargained for as he set about spelling *Croc Eadar Dha Ghreuch*, i.e. a mountain between two mountain pastures, with Cassidy by his side alternately helping him or criticising his efforts, No, No not C R U C, CROC etc. Mrs. Madden the wife of the landlord came out while this was going on and then went in to report to the company assembled for dinner that one of the tennants from the mountain was teaching Lord Erne how to spell.

O'Donovan is now about to bid farewell to Maguire's county and writes his last letter in the county in Enniskillen on Monday night the 24th of December, Christmas Eve, 1834. He makes a few passing references to Fermanagh in later letters and in particular wrote on February 27th 1835 linking incidents in the Annals of the Four Masters and the Book of Invasions to locations in Fermanagh. He also comments on the propensity of the peasants of Fermanagh to mispronounce M and B as in Lismellaw instead of Lisbellaw or Munone instead of Bunone and again this is something that one does still hear occasionally even today.

With this remark on the diction of County Fermanagh the active involvement of John O'Donovan with County Fermanagh at least for the purposes of the Ordnance Survey virtually ceases apart from a few other references in later letters from other counties. He has traversed on foot almost every inch of the Fermanagh taking notes, talking, arguing and conversing, and teasing from the old mountain folk the ancient stories of the county of Fermanagh. In effect, he took the tales of the Annals to the only people who were still able to understand them, and who could add to them, especially in relation to location. We owe an incredible debt of gratitude to this truly active historian who defied the dogs of the country as well as the turkeys and the geese to give us what was in effect our last last glimpse of the ancient Kingdoms of County Fermanagh.

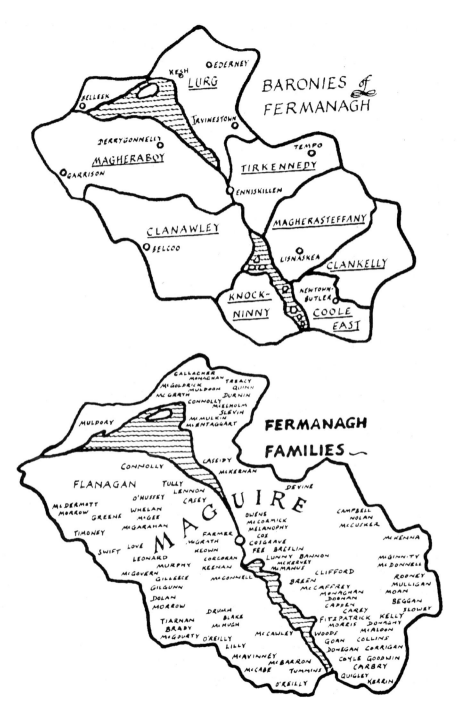

BARONIES of FERMANAGH

LURG
O EDERNEY
KESH
BELLEEK O
IRVINESTOWN
DERRYGONNELLY O
MAGHERABOY
O GARRISON
TEMPO O
TIRKENNEDY
ENNISKILLEN O
CLANAWLEY
MAGHERASTEFFANY
O BELCOO
LISNASKEA O
CLANKELLY
KNOCK-
NINNY
NEWTOWN-
BUTLER O
COOLE
EAST

FERMANAGH
FAMILIES

GALLACHER
MONAGHAN TREACY
McGOLDRICK MULDOON QUINN
McGRATH DURNIN
CONNOLLY
MCELHOLM
SLEVIN
McMULKIN
McENTAGGART
MULDORY
CONNOLLY CASSIDY
McKERNAN
FLANAGAN TULLY DEVINE
LENNON
D'HUSSEY CASEY
McDERMOTT WHELAN
MORROW GREENE McGEE
McGARAHAN
TIMONEY OWENS CAMPBELL
McCORMICK NOLAN
SWIFT LOVE MELANOPHY McCUSKER
COX
FARMER COSGRAVE
McGRATH FEE BRESLIN McKENNA
KEOWN LUNNY BANNON
LEONARD CORCORAN McKERVEY McGINNITY
MURPHY KEENAN McMANUS McDONNELL
McGOVERN McCONNELL CLIFFORD ROONEY
GILLEECE BREEN MULLIGAN
GILGUNN McCAFFREY MOAN
DOLAN MONAGHAN BEGGAN
MORROW DOOHAN
DRUMM CAPPEN CAREY SLOWEY
TIARNAN BLAKE FITZPATRICK KELLY
BRADY McHUGH MORRIS DONAGHY
McGOURTY O'REILLY McCAULEY WOODS McALOON
LILLY GOAN COLLINS
McAVINNEY DONEGAN CORRIGAN
McBARRON COYLE GOODWIN
McCABE TUMMINS CARBRY
O'REILLY QUIGLEY KERRIN

MAGUIRE

39

Thomas Drummond, R.E., F.R.A.S., (1797-1840)
Surveyor and Administrator

A.J. Malley

During the early nineteenth century one of the most able of the surveyors to be sent to Ireland to assist Lt. Col. Colby with the new survey was Thomas Drummond. Although well known in map making circles, Drummond is famous in Ireland for other reasons, including the invention of 'limelight', used in lighthouses; the formation of an effective police force in Ireland; and as Head of the Boundary Commission and of the Railway Commission. He was also to show his ability in fair government as Under-Secretary to the Lord Lieutenant of Ireland for five years.

Thomas Drummond was born on the 10th October 1797 in Edinburgh, his father being James Drummond, a member of the Society of writers to the Signet and his mother, Elizabeth Somers, a lady noted or her beauty and character. His father died when Drummond was only three years old, leaving Mrs. Drummond to bring up four young children. Drummond proved to be a brilliant scholar. Mr. Scott, a former teacher, recollected in 1812 that, 'His knowledge of geometry, I have never seen equalled in one of his years and the progress he is now making in the higher branches of mathematics and natural philosophy, is such as might be expected from one who possesses a sound judgement combined with uncommon application.' He entered Edinburgh University at the age of

Thomas Drummond
(1797-1840)

thirteen and Professor Leslie said of him, 'No young man has ever come under my charge with a happier disposition or more promising talents'. Professor Jardine also thought him to be 'one of the cleverest boys' at the University.

He showed a keen interest in inventing things from an early age and his sister noted that he was always busy about the house 'making things'. His mother is recorded as saying of him that 'about the house his power of contrivance made him exceedingly useful and whatever went wrong, from the roasting jack upwards, the appeal to Tommy was to put it right'. The interest in inventing things never left him.

In 1812, at the age of fifteen, Thomas Drummond became a cadet at the Royal Military Academy, Woolwich. His interest in being an engineer is evident in a letter he wrote to a friend, Mr. Aitchison, on the 3rd October 1812, 'I feel a strong inclination for the profession of a military engineer. I have studied for these two years for such a line and have received a satisfactory certificate from Mr. Leslie, Professor of Mathematics in Edinburgh. Could I only be so fortunate as to obtain a strong recommendation to Lord Mulgrave, I would soon obtain the wished-for appointment'. Just how determined Drummond was is shown by the following incident which occurred at Woolwich. He was to take an examination in February 1813 at 11.00 a.m. and instructed the steward to call him early in the morning so that he could catch the coach. The steward forgot and Drummond rose at 7.00 a.m. and reached shore to find that the coach has left ten minutes earlier. He decided to give chase and ran after it for three miles but failed to overtake it. Luckily a chaise came along and he obtained a lift to within two miles of Woolwich. After running the rest of the way he arrived with five minutes to spare, sat the examination and passed with flying colours!

He does not appear to have been entirely happy at Woolwich but his constant success in studies kept him going. He soon passed up the grades and in one year jumped up fifty-five places. By 1813 he was in third academy, later that year passing into the second and by early 1814 had graduated to the first. In July 1815 he obtained a Commission in the Royal Engineers at the age of eighteen. While he was at Chatham, his first posting, he invented a form of floating pontoon which was capable of being dismantled and carried on horseback. This was very well thought of by his fellow officers.

Lt. Col. T.F. Colby (1784-1852) Director of the Ordnance Survey

In July 1818 Drummond was stationed at Edinburgh but he soon found it boring and decided to abandon the army for the law. He entered his name at Lincoln's Inn, London. Fortunately he met, in 1819, Lt. Col. Thomas F.

Colby, who was working with the Ordnance Survey in Scotland. When Colby was appointed Superintendent of the Survey in 1820, Drummond was persuaded to join the Ordnance Survey and over the following years, worked closely with Colby in surveys of Kent, Surrey and Hertford.

By 1823 the British Survey was dropped in favour of the Irish Survey proposed to assist with the new valuation of property in Ireland, based on the townland rather than the farm. In 1824 the Select Committee under Mr. Thomas Spring Rice sat to discuss the method of surveying Ireland at the new scale of six inches to the

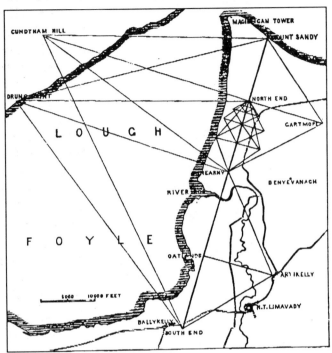

Base Line, Magilligan, Co. Derry
1827-1828

mile. The Survey was to commence in the north and work south. In order to achieve very accurate measurements, a very accurately measured base line was required from which all the triangles would be based. Colby chose to lay down this base line in the Magilligan area as it was flat and was close to Scotland and could therefore be connected to their survey lines. Drummond was working closely with Colby on this task but had reservations about the quality of lights used to pinpoint hill tops on which the surveyors focussed the large 36 inch theodolites. The lamps they had been using were not very powerful and were especially weak in murky conditions.

Drummond was convinced he could improve on the lights and in 1823, while in London, he attended the lectures of Brande and Faraday at the Royal Institution and noted that they had suggested that lime could be used to enhance

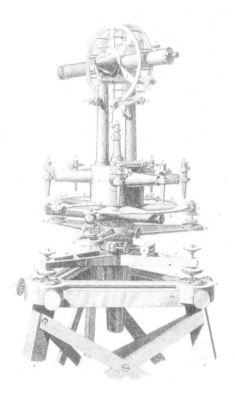

Example of a Large Theodolite

a flame burning. He decided to experiment and produce his own lamp and reflector and so he set up his lamp on Knocklayd mountain in County Antrim for observers to see from Divis mountain, a distance of forty miles. The light was clearly seen and a 'shout of exultation' came from a crowd of civilian onlookers as they observed the brilliant light. Later, in 1825, during October and November, Drummond and his light moved to Slieve Snaght in County Donegal, some 67 miles from Divis mountain. The distance was so great that a second smaller lamp was set up on the church tower at Randalstown in the line of sight to try to guide the observers. Drummond's diary tells of the hardships they had to endure on Slieve Snaght and extracts are as follows –

28th October 1825	'The tent is now up and in a few minutes the wall around it will be completed ... the fog still continues.'
4th November 1825	'A storm of snow came on at that hour (2.13 p.m.) ... my tent is blown down and I now write from a kind of cave formed on the lee side of the hill.'
8th November 1825	'Squall succeeded squall'
11th November 1825	'3 a.m. The poor devil who went for the letters has been wandering on the hills since five in the evening.'
12th November 1825	'At last we had nothing remaining but the lamp tent and the walls of the cooking house.'

It was later on that day that the news was received from Divis that the light had got through. The lamp was used for most of the other observations in Ireland and therefore speeded up the triangulation of Ireland.

43

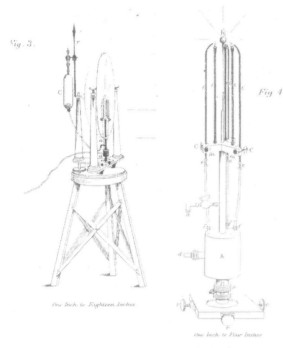

One Inch to Eighteen Inches

Fig. 4

One Inch to Four Inches

Drummond's Lamp, 1826

Drummond also invented his version of the heliostat for use in connection with the observation from hill tops, and again it speeded up the surveyor's work. The beam of light from Drummond's light was so strong that he suggested that it be used in lighthouses and so he made larger versions with special reflectors. At the trials in 1830 all three main lamps were used and when Drummond's light was shown it was so overpowering that 'a shout of triumph and of admiration burst from all present'. Colby also wrote in 1830, that in an experiment he witnessed, the light, although ten miles away, was able to cast a shadow of his finger on a white sheet of paper. The success of Drummond's light in lighthouses was undoubtedly the saviour of many lives and his statue by Hogan in the City Hall in Dublin depicts him with a lighthouse beside him. The use of lime burning in the flame was to become better known in the world of stage and theatre because stage lighting also made use of the principle, hence the phrase 'to be in the limelight'.

Drummond was also to assist Colby in the measurement of the base line at Lough Foyle, which was to be the line from which all other survey lines were to be measured. This meant that it had to be accurate and so Colby devised a set of Compensation Bars and with the assistance of Drummond refined the bars to be extremely accurate. The principle employed was that a bar of iron 10 feet 1.5 inches long connected to a bar of brass of the same length. This meant that even if the temperature rose or fell, the point at which they were hinged remained the same. Six bars were used and they were placed on trestles and covered by tents to shade them from the sun. Each bar was joined to the next and lined up precisely to tiny dots by means of microscopes. The line was

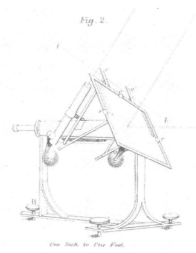

Fig. 2.

One Inch to One Foot.

Drummond's Heliostat

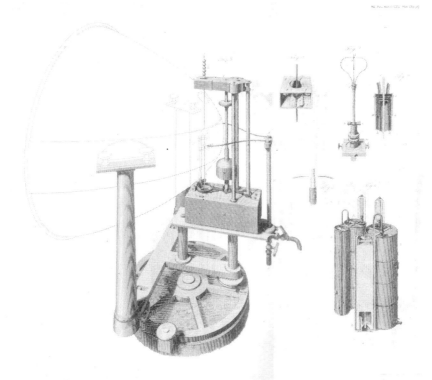

Drummond's Light as used in Lighthouses, 1830

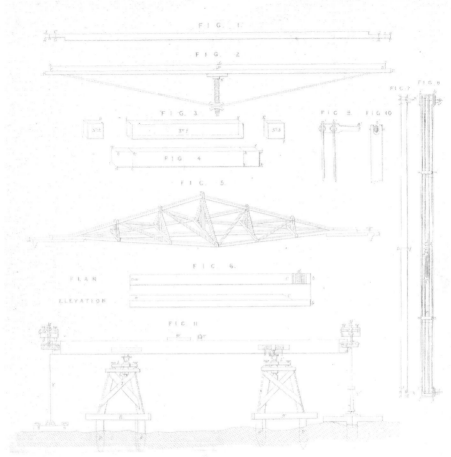

Compensation Bars used to measure the Base Line
Magilligan to Ballykelly, Co. Derry 1827-1828

started at a point at Magilligan beach and a low tower marked the spot until recently. It continued in a straight line towards Ballykelly village where the end tower still stands, a gun barrel buried in the centre marking the end point. The line measured 41,640.8873 feet or 7.89 miles and it included a crossing of the River Roe, a distance of some 450 feet. The original length was remeasured in 1960 using modern equipment and was found to be only one inch out.

The survey of the base line in 1827 and 1828 took sixty days of work with a complement of seventy men under the direction of Captain Thomas Drummond. The actual map of the base line and all its detail is still extant in the archives of the Ordnance Survey in Belfast. One of the compensation bars

Statue of Thomas Drummond with Lighthouse by Hogan
1843 City hall, Dublin

47

1827-1828

is still in the Ordnance Survey Office in Dublin. In 1831 Drummond left the Ordnance Survey to concentrate on his invention of the lamp for use in lighthouses. He presented his drawings etc. to King William IV who was very impressed. He was to meet Lord Brougham, the Lord Chancellor, later that year and soon was given the post of the Head of Boundary Commission. In 1833 he became private secretary to Lord Althorp, Chancellor of the Exchequer and in 1835 was to return to Ireland as Under-Secretary at Dublin Castle. While in office he administered the country with great wisdom, firmness and justice

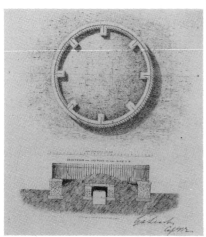

Base Tower at each end of Base Line. Magilligan/Ballykelly

and soon became very popular. He was noted for his organisation of the police force and for his refusal to force Roman Catholics to pay Tithes. In 1838 the Tithe Commutation Act was passed and that Act reformed the old system. Drummond also devised schemes to assist the poor in Ireland and suggested a Railway Commission be set up which he presided over.

On the 19th November 1835, at the age of thirty eight, Drummond married a wealthy heiress, Miss Maria Kinnaird, and they had three daughters, Mary Elizabeth, Emily and Fanny. His wife took a great interest in his work but also complained that the family never saw much of him as he was always working. By 1838 Drummond had been over-working and became ill and by 1839 his health became so bad that he was forced to take a short leave of absence. He returned to work in February 1840 and continued to work long hours, eventually becoming seriously ill on Sunday, 12th April 1840 and dying three days later. He was buried on the 21st April in Mount Jerome Cemetery, Dublin and the funeral was so large that over 150 carriages attended. The chief mourner was Daniel O'Connell. Carved on Drummond's monument are his final words – 'Bury me in Ireland, the land of my adoption. I have loved her well and served her faithfully'. So died one of Ireland's most skilful administrators and surveyors, but at least Thomas Drummond will be remembered for his contribution to map making, lighthouses and limelight, and for the five years of relative peace which occurred under his administration, so it is therefore fitting that Mount Drummond Gardens in Dublin and Drummond Park in Derry should be named after him.

Thomas Drummond's Monument
Mount Jerome Cemetery, Dublin

49

Sources

1. 'On the Illumination of Light-houses' by Lieut. Thomas Drummond, June 1830.
2. 'Memoir of Thomas Drummond' by John F. McLennan, 1867.
3. 'Memoir of the life of Major-General Colby' by Lt. Col. J.E. Portlock, 1869.
4. 'Thomas Drummond – Life and Letters' by R. Harry O'Brien, 1889.
5. Londonderry Standard – 14:4:1840; 22:4:1840; 29:4:1840.
6. Londonderry Sentinel – 18:4:1840; 2:5:1840.
7. Belfast Newsletter – 17:4:1840.
8. The Dictionary of National Biography.
9. 'The Early Years of The Ordnance Survey' by Col. Sir Charles Close.
10. 'Thomas Drummond' by Laurence O'Dea, Dublin Historical Record, Vol. XXIV, 1970-71.
11. 'The Ordnance Survey of Ireland' by Commandant P.G. Madden, The Irish Sword.
12. 'A Paper Landscape – The Ordnance Survey in Nineteenth Century Ireland' by J.H. Andrews, 1975.
13. 'Ordnance Survey in Ireland – An Illustrated Record' by Staff of the Ordnance Survey, Dublin and Belfast, 1991.

Acknowledgement is given for the assistance of Leonard Hinds, Ordnance Survey, Dublin and Mary Clarke, City Hall Archives, Dublin.

ACE Map (Address Centred Extract Map) – A New Service from Ordnance Survey of Northern Ireland

S. Gray

What is ACE Map? To fully understand this exciting and innovatory service recently introduced by Ordnance Survey of Northern Ireland (OSNI) one must look back to 1981 when this organization, as the government body responsible for the official survey and mapping of Northern Ireland, commenced a feasibility study to establish the benefits of replacing conventional map production with a computerized system.

The plan, subsequently implemented in the mid 1980s aims to complete digital conversion of the survey archive into a sophisticated fully structured, topographic database before the end of the 1990s and even more significantly, to use the inherent geographic reference facility as the common link in producing a distributed but integrated geographic information system for Northern Ireland – NIGIS. All major government and public utilities are involved in development of the latter and Liaison Committees representing partners with interests as diverse as environment, agriculture,

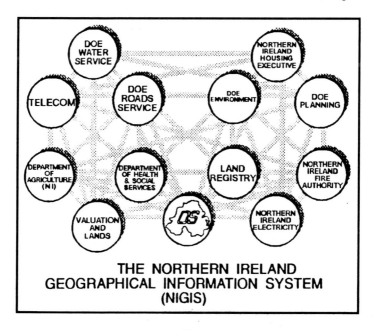

THE NORTHERN IRELAND
GEOGRAPHICAL INFORMATION SYSTEM
(NIGIS)

telecommunications and electricity supply, ensure co-operation towards interaction between their respective spatially referenced data holdings.

Both projects are being progressed with the OSNI topographic database the more advanced, data being input from both large-scale 1:1250/1:2500 and small scale 1:50 000/1:250 000 mapping. The large-scale database contains fully structured digital data, all maps sheets being edge-matched and with associated textual information linked to the map graphic. Data is up to date at initial conversion and once databased comes immediately under a digital maintenance programme.

In addition to its role in serving the ever increasing demand for accurate and up-to-date digital topographical data the database is improving the efficiency and enhancing the flexibility of the printed map service. With a large proportion of data within the NIGIS environment having the postal address as its spatial reference, eventual inclusion within NIGIS is being facilitated by OSNI linking the postal address to each addressable property in the database through a system generated Irish Grid Reference.

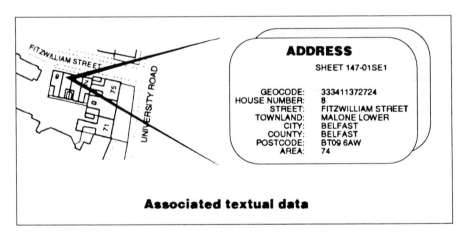

This in turn has enabled introduction of ACE Map where upon entry of a customer supplied postal address or Irish Grid reference an up-to-date large scale map extract, centred on the specified location, can be output.

The significant features of the new service are:

• freedom from the constraints of map sheet lines inherent in the traditional paper-based system, often a source of inconvenience and additional expense when a particular property or location fell on the junction of possibly up to four map sheets.

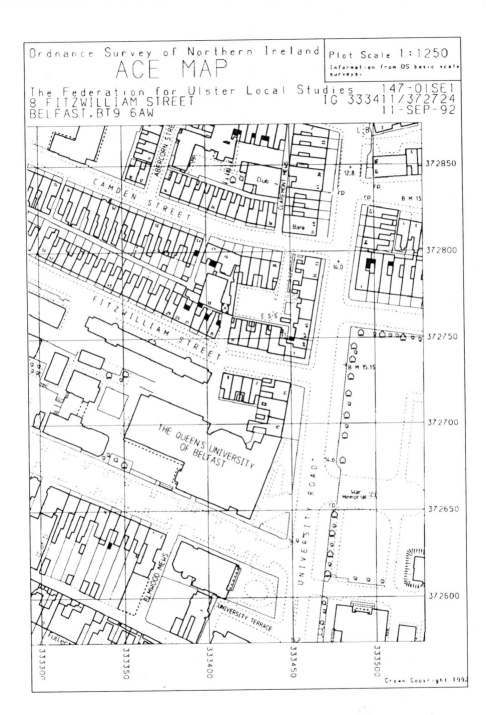

- customer selected location with address, Irish Grid reference, the relevant map sheet number, and, if desired, the customer's name, included.
- up-to-date information content thus overcoming the old problem of paper map stocks becoming out-of-date.
- map extract selection by postal address or twelve figure Irish Grid reference.
- extract size presently A4 but with extended options possible in the light of user demand.
- output scales presently offered 1:500, 1:1250 and 1:2500. Here again the range will be expanded if demand is evident. Regardless of scale of output data accuracy is that applicable to the basic scale of survey for the area requested.
- keenly priced, currently £7.00 per extract, with additional prints of any extract, if requested with order, £2.00 per print.
- available now for the Belfast City and Castlereagh district, being extended to include more of Greater Belfast by the end of 1992 and the remainder of Northern Ireland in line with the continuing digital conversion programme.
- small orders normally as you wait service, larger orders overnight service. Orders accepted at map sales counter or by fax or post.
- available from Map Sales, Ordnance Survey of Northern Ireland, Colby House, Stranmillis Court, Belfast, BT9 5BJ. ☎ 0232 661244 or Fax 0232 683211.

The service is fast, automated and ideally suited to any operation where large-scale map information is essential. It has numerous applications within the public and private sector and has particular relevance to property conveyancing and certification, planning applications, incident recording (e.g. road accidents, insurance claims, etc.), localized mapping for public utility purposes or for central depiction of features of specialist or scientific interest. The competitive price and currency of information are major benefits, not only to the professional in reducing costs and improving service to clients, but also to the private individual or organization where flexibility in defining the extent must be a major saving.

Possibly the first of its kind in Europe, it puts OSNI to the fore in the application of digital technology to the provision of a personalized mapping service, which in combination with other OSNI digital services available is ensuring full exploitation of the technology for the benefit of all in Northern Ireland.

Ballymena's Ecclesiastical Antiquary: William Reeves (1815-92)

E. Dunlop

In accordance with his usual custom Dr. Reeves began at once to collect materials for a history of the parish.

(Lady Ferguson)

Given the truth of this remark, made in a hastily-assembled *Life* (1893) of the great friend of the author's late husband, the invitation to offer a centenary review of even some of the achievements of William Reeves is not one lightly to be taken up. At best, and within the present small compass, it is possible to highlight only certain areas of his work, which then deserve more specialist analysis under other auspices. As for our opening quotation, it was made in relation to Lusk, County Dublin, where Reeves became vicar late in 1857. But the present interest is in Reeves' activities and achievements in the preceding period, which began in 1841, with the appointment of this remarkable man as incumbent of Kilconriola (Ballymena), County Antrim.

(i) "Apud villam mediam": incumbent of Kilconriola (1841-57)

… Ballymena [is] the second town in size and importance in the county, and one of the most extensive linen and flax markets in the North. The town itself, although much improved of late, has no pretensions to architectural beauty, or picturesqueness of situation…

When J.B. Doyle, in the 1850s, wrote up his impressions of the North of Ireland, he was frank in his comments about the various sights which had greeted him. And, quite obviously, Mid-Antrim had been found to be visually deficient. Despite Ballymena's obvious prosperity in the middle of the nineteenth century, Doyle firmly rejected the town's claims to aesthetic fame. For a very different reason, however, Doyle still found Ballymena worthy of note. "The present incumbent is the Rev. Dr. William Reeves, the accomplished author."

Born on 16 March 1815, in the same year and in the same county of Cork as his friend, Robert King (see below), William Reeves, also like King, was a graduate of Trinity College, Dublin, who was at one stage (in Reeves' case, 1848-58) headmaster of the Diocesan School of Armagh and Connor, the somewhat eccentric antecedent (1828) of Ballymena Academy. And it was the portrait of Reeves (reproduced above), hanging in the former premises in Thomas Street and then in the new school (1967) at Knockanure, which first encouraged a schoolboy's interest in the churchman's very considerable achievements. As recently as 1990, the historic Diocesan School and its several additions, lately occupied by civil servants, were demolished in favour of making Ballymena even more of what Jack McCann has called, with more than a little regret, a 'supermarket town'. But the visitor, walking the congested streets of modern Ballymena, one hundred and fifty-one years after Reeves' first settlement in this parish, discovers that the erstwhile incumbent is not left without a memorial. Planted four-square, at the head of Castle Street, and on the approximate site of a landlord's much earlier mansion than that of the later 1860s (which was demolished in the 1950s), is the new parish church of St. Patrick's. Consecrated by Bishop Knox on 2 August 1855, its foundation stone having been laid on 17 March 1853, this edifice was the long-awaited response

St. Patrick's Parish Church

to a painfully evident need. Since the Rev. Hugh Smyth Cumming, the local man who later moved to Loughinisland, County Down, had succeeded the ineffectual Rev. Richard Babington as curate in 1820, a steady decline in the Episcopalian cause had been reversed, with the result that the old parish church, quietly located off Church Street, had soon become inadequate. Thus Reeves, despite his general magnanimity reported by Lady Ferguson, was more than keen to effect some denominational reassertion in a town where, he alleged in his *Memoir of the Church of Ballymena* (1854), the "Church people of the parish, who [once] numbered but some half-dozen families" had sometimes lived by "a sort of sufferance among the great mass of the Presbyterian population". There is more than a little irony, then, in the fact that the project

faltered financially and was secured only by the enduring support of the Adairs, lords of the soil and descendants of the seventeenth-century Presbyterian who

The grave of Emma Reeves

had crossed from the vicinity of Portpatrick to acquire land in Mid-Antrim and to sponsor the growth of 'the middle town'.

While it has been a source of pleasure in the Reeves centenary year to see the erection, by Ballymena Borough Council, of a commemorative plaque on the tower of St. Patrick's, two items within the church deserve the visitor's notice. First, one of the memorials to the Casement family, who had not yet been overtaken by controversy. It was after Francis Casement that Reeves' ninth child (born on 30 September 1855) was named, a child whose mother did not long survive. Thus another memorial, a window commemorating Emma Reeves, whose funeral service on 16 October was, by sad coincidence, the first to be held in St. Patrick's. The grave of Mrs. Reeves may be seen behind the tower (all that remains) of the old parish church, where, despite Reeves himself being buried in Armagh, the headstone also takes account of his presidency of the Royal Irish Academy in the last year of his life. We are therefore reminded that the antiquarian interests which had been evident from his school-days provided Reeves with some small measure of solace in his last few years in Ballymena. But that measure was sometimes small indeed. Hear him on 25 November 1856, as he completed the preface to his edition of Adamnan's *Life of Columba*. While testifying to "many hours of genuine happiness in social or epistolary intercourse with dear and highly-valued friends on either side of the channel", which contributed to "many seasons of relief from the sorrows of a troubled mind", he was still, as he said, a "man of two portions". And yet his *Columba* was a most authoritative work, arguably the *apogée* of a rigorous programme of study which had borne its first fruits within three years of Reeves' arrival in Ballymena.

(ii) "The driest details of topography and chronology"

Dr. Reeves joins to the solidity and accuracy of Camden a charm peculiar to himself, by which the driest details of topography and chronology are made delightful. There is not a parish, scarcely a townland, in the counties of Derry, Down and Antrim, over which he has not breathed an air from the ancient humanities, which imparts picturesqueness and animation to what used to be one of the bleakest fields of investigation in all the circuit of Ireland.

Here it was the turn of Sir Samuel Ferguson himself to pass admiring comment. The lawyer, poet and archivist, whom Reeves, as Bishop of Connor, would see interred (1886) in the churchyard at Donegore, was paying tribute to his friend's great industry, which still impresses the modern reader, whatever his native townland, of J.B. Garstin's detailed Bibliography (1893).

It would appear that Reeves' first published work was his paper on "Nendrum, commonly called Mahee Island", read before the Down and Connor Church Architecture Society (of which more below) in 1844, published in the following year and republished as late as 1902. But, having exchanged Blaris (where, it is worthy of notice, he had had timely experience of 'church extension' at Broomhedge) for more northerly Ballymena, Reeves naturally became deeply interested in the antiquities of Mid-Antrim. As there exist fragments about the parish of Ballyclug (which lies directly across the Braid from Ballymena), so there is also extant a manuscript 'Memoir of the Parish of Kilconriola' (1845). Now proposed for publication at an early date, by Braid Books and the Dunclug Press, that item, preserved in a notebook which later had its own interesting history, had also been read before the Church Architecture Society.

While it is intended that the forthcoming publication will discuss in detail the status of the 'Memoir' within the local historical encyclopaedia, two points from its pages have already proved useful. (1) First, when Professor J.H. Andrews was preparing his commentary on the Linen Hall Library's edition (1987) of James Lendrick's map (1780) of County Antrim, there was renewed proof of the importance of transcribing memorials. A newspaper cutting, provenance unknown, had suggested that the cartographer was commemorated in Ballymena's old churchyard. While a very recent survey of the graves had yielded no such detail, it was satisfying eventually to be able to relay to Professor Andrews the words (*Hic in solo natale conduntur ossa Iacobi Lendrick, ob iv Sept AD 1800, aet 57 an. Hoc marmor filii posuere.*) which had

The Old Churchyard, Ballymena

long ago been transcribed by the historically-minded incumbent. Moreover, Reeves' sketch made it possible to identify the niche on the church tower from which the tablet had vanished. (2) Then there was his note that "the shops were first lit by gas" on 22 November 1842 and that "the streets were also lit in like manner" on 23 August 1843; this has made possible the marking of a municipal sesquicentenary in this year of 1992.

These are indeed important local details, but the 'Memoir' was only an earnest of that which was to come. Within two years Reeves would produce a much more substantial work, dealing with far more than a single parish.

(iii) "Can these bones live?"

Perhaps the most remarkable thing about this work is the manner in which Reeves has made use of an ancient taxation-list as the basis of a volume replete with information and interest of every kind ... "Son of man, can these bones live?" Reeves believed they could: and he proceeded to clothe the skeleton with flesh and blood, so that after six hundred years' mouldering decay it revived and stood upright.

If J.E.L. Oulton, then Regius Professor of Divinity in the University of Dublin, believed that his memorial discourse (24 May 1937) on 'William Reeves, Bishop, Scholar, Antiquary' would be seen to have been all too indebted to Lady Ferguson's encomium of some forty-four years before, his clever appropriation of an image from Ezekiel 37 would still have been sufficient to justify a piece which was, of course, most stylish throughout. For Oulton had identified exactly the character of Reeves' great achievement in the years up to 1847. As his own Introduction to *The Ecclesiastical Antiquities of Down, Connor and Dromore* makes clear, the incumbent of Kilconriola was wont to immerse himself in the archiepiscopal record closet and other repositories. Thus the nature of the *Antiquities*, which is, in fact, a much annotated edition (xxiv + 436 pages) of a diocesan taxation of 1306.

But what was the purpose behind its appearance? Had the taxation simply provided, as Reeves once remarked, an excuse for publishing a book, a peg upon which to hang multifarious other material? Despite such learned levity, we cannot overlook contemporary controversy, given that Richard Mant, the prelate to whom Reeves was greatly devoted, was the much-lauded dedicatee of a work which would serve as a kind of diocesan handbook. It was "the companion of [Mant's] journey", which progress had had its own times of difficulty. Fundamental to one episode was the outlook of the Church Architecture Society, a body founded in October 1842, whose president was Mant and whose purpose was to promote "the beauty of holiness", though entirely without "superstitious admixture". By February 1843, some laymen, in association with the Rev. Thomas Drew (sometime of Broughshane and Loughinisland), had memorialised Mant, believing the new body to be an Irish equivalent of the suspect Cambridge Camden Society, likely to spread abroad what they held to be the pernicious influence of the *Tracts for the Times*. The diocesan protested that his own attitude towards Rome had always been clear and that the Society's motives were similarly open and pure. Nevertheless, Mant eventually resigned as a patron of the Camden Society, a body with which the Church Architecture Society also felt that it should no longer officially communicate. Indeed the Irish organisation would eventually re-title itself the Harris Society (in honour of the antiquary, Walter Harris), thus attempting to emphasise its strictly historical purposes. And here Reeves may well have been influential, given some correspondence with Mant in the difficult year of 1843, which is quoted by Lady Ferguson. Before Reeves had long been settled in Ballymena, he had set before his bishop acceptable proposals concerning, in Mant's words, "the attainment of general information as to the ecclesiastical topography of the diocese". This agenda (coinciding with Mant's own outlook, "rather perhaps going beyond it") may have been timely, making possible, if it was not already so, "an enlargement of the Society's objects" at that period of no little dispute.

And how had the *Antiquities* been put together? "In the compilation of the Notes and Appendix, the writer has endeavoured to consult for their accuracy by a personal examination of the existing antiquarian remains in the three dioceses." What may be said of Reeves' topographical intentions? His friend, J.H. Todd, Regius Professor of Hebrew in the University of Dublin, certainly saw this diocesan project as being ultimately one of theological reclamation from Rome, an attempt to open the eyes of the people, "to make them see its vast importance, not only in attaching to the Church its own members, but also in bringing others to see our real claims and our true position, as the Church of Patrick, Bridget and Columcille, and the only Church that possesses their true 'Comharbas'". Here is a particular view of Irish ecclesiastical history, the dogmatic promotion of the Reformed Catholic Church, as the Rev. Robert King, Reeves' successor in the Diocesan School, was to call it. For many modern readers of the *Antiquities*, however, the greater interest must lie in the local historical detail which had been amassed by Reeves. As well as the many detailed footnotes to the main text, in this complex work which would test all the ingenuity of the modern typesetter, there are thirty-six appendices, on topographical and other entities from Rathlin to Mourne, which amount to three-quarters of the volume. In all a veritable quarry. And what of nomenclature? "The modern names of the parishes and townlands are given according to the orthography adopted by the Ordnance Survey, from which boundless store of modern topography the writer has liberally drawn..." To the matter of official publications we shall presently return.

Meanwhile, was there some truth in J.B. Doyle's later suggestion that Reeves had proposed a "parochial history" of Ireland? Having thus dealt with the area east of the Bann by 1847, Reeves next did something similar for the

Diocese of Derry, in respect of an item which had been noted in the Introduction to the *Antiquities*. His annotated edition (xx + 149 pages) of the *Acts of Archbishop Colton in his Metropolitan Visitation* of 1397, with a *Rental of the See Estates at the time* appeared in 1850. Once again a Latin text was amplified by many details of interest to the modern student of local topography. Moreover there are also valuable insights into Reeves' way of working. Thus, on page 49, the communication, to a tireless correspondent, from the late rector of Banagher and Dungiven about "the most aboriginal clan of McCloskys [sic]" being found in the townland of Cluntgeerah. And Reeves also had a correspondent who took a polemical interest in the ruined church "on the N[orth] side of the Moyola, in Moneyconey, one of the 'six towns' of Ballynascreen". It was around those ruins that Robert King, from 1845 to 1851 the district curate of St. Anne's, Sixtowns, built his highly imaginative, because disarmingly conversational, case about what he believed to be the true Catholic Church of Ireland. But, as already noted, it was Reeves, not King, who, having paid some attention in this *Visitation* to Adamnan and Columba, would apply further critical scrutiny to the mediaeval texts. And it happened in Ballymena, a place which hardly deserved such eminence, according to a reviewer (thought to be John Scott Porter), who, in relation to Reeves' edition of Adamnan's *Columba* (1857), offered a kind of congratulation to the Established Church "which [could] afford to employ such a man in the obscure labours of the curacy of Kilconriola".

Even if we assume that Porter's own Remonstrant reasons for seeing the limitations of Ballymena (where certain Presbyterians had lately taken exception to Subscription) in some way coloured his judgment, there is still much in his assertion. In the *Antiquities* Reeves himself had depicted his location as archivally disadvantageous ("a hundred miles from Dublin and in the midst of parochial engagements, which allowed of only occasional snatches for making the necessary inquiries"), but he was one of a wider côterie dedicated to the study of antiquities. For example, John O'Donovan, the first professor (1849) of Celtic Languages in Queen's College, Belfast, and formerly field-worker of the Ordnance Survey, was his frequent guest in Ballymena (*pace* the location, by the visitor's recent biographer, of Reeves in Ballymoney). And this leads us neatly to the alphabetical index of townlands, an item upon which Reeves had been working since 1853, in a field to which he had been sensitive for a far longer period of time. As he explained in "On the Townland Distribution of Ireland", a paper (1861) to the Royal Irish Academy, his two volumes (which contained 1560 pages with more than 62,000 entries) had more or less coincided with an official publication. But how had this come about, especially since the community of scholars was of limited size and since one of Reeves' "literary friends", who particularly benefited from the "monster Index" was, according to Lady Ferguson, none other than the eminent O'Donovan? At least, according to the author's note on the Linen Hall Library's copy which was used, with gratitude, for a modern reprint (1992) of the 1861 paper, Sir Thomas Larcom had given Reeves the opportunity to write the Introduction to the official *Townland Index*. But he who often stole hours from the night had "declined the work from want of time". And we must believe him. Nevertheless, while protesting the inferiority of his own volumes, which have been lodged in the Bodleian since November 1892, Reeves had still documented their existence and had exhibited, moreover, his special knowledge of their subject. To handle Reeves' Index in the solemnity of Duke Humfrey, in 1991, was to take a certain pride in the fact that it had been completed (1857) in Ballymena and, at the same time, to be so chauvinistic as to check that the ancestral townlands of Ballymacveigh [sic] and Tullynamullan, in the parish of Connor, had not been forgotten.

By his forty-second birthday Reeves had indeed done well, albeit amidst personal tragedy. But one literary project would for ever defeat him, an edition of the Book of Armagh, the text which he himself had purchased for the Church of Ireland at a time when the Primate, Beresford, had hesitated. Over the years Reeves knew great frustration with that major literary and historical project, but he simply could not get it completed. Might not a change of location have helped?

(iv) Reeves after Ballymena

It was J.H. Todd, of Trinity College, Dublin (where, over the years, Reeves had been an unsuccessful applicant for various academic positions), who, as Treasurer of St. Patrick's, Dublin, offered a more studious location than Ballymena. "Lusk is classical ground for Irish antiquities, and is only twenty minutes distant from Dublin by the Drogheda Railway", a prospect that before the end of 1857 resulted in Reeves' removal from the curacy of Kilconriola (although he did not leave the Diocesan School until the summer of 1858). If the Glebe House at Lusk, now a private dwelling, has a pleasant enough setting, it must still have been a considerable change, even for one who welcomed a quieter life and easy access to the literary resources of Trinity, to switch from the sheer cathedrality of St. Patrick's in Ballymena to the much smaller parish church (1847) built on to the round tower of Lusk. And yet the overall appearance of the edifice at Lusk is most striking. The church whose predecessor had lost its roof in the Big Wind of 1839, is raised from the plain by a belfry which adds three towers to the larger, tenth-century erection and which contains memorials of the Barnewall and St. Lawrence families. For the record, that church now houses a folk museum dedicated to the memory of Willie Monks, a local historian. Is it not imperative, however, that on that site there should also be some memorial to the antiquary who occupied the building for its original spiritual purpose?

It was noted at the outset that soon after arrival in Lusk Reeves set about discovering the parochial history, as he also did when he became rector of Tynan in 1865. From 1861 he had been Keeper of the unique institution that is Archbishop Robinson's Public Library in Armagh, with a curate taking care of Lusk during the week. Rural Dean as well as Librarian, Reeves could hardly have been better placed, if apart from Trinity, to exercise his skills, as his truly impressive index (4 vols.) in Armagh still shows. As has already been demonstrated, he had a special penchant for such doggedly detailed work, a point also illustrated by his having indexed the *Works* of Josephus while in Lisburn and having completed and indexed Elrington's *Ussher*. In this later period of his life, however, Reeves produced papers rather than books. It was left to another to bring forth, as late as 1913, an edition of the Book of Armagh.

After more than two decades among the literary treasures of the ecclesiastical capital, and at an age when he deserved even more splendid retiral, our subject was suddenly thrust into the world. How, then, did the bookish Reeves, who became Bishop of Down & Connor & Dromore (rather than Primate) in 1886, fare as prelate? The suggestion of C.F. D'Arcy, a more recent Primate who had been his successor in both Ballymena and in the bishopric, that it was almost cruel to send the scholarly septuagenarian into the overwhelming business of Belfast and environs, finds some hectic support in cordial but urgent correspondence to an old colleague. Is it then insensitively glib to wonder if, in that final period of not a little academic frustration, Reeves took some deserved solace in the *Ecclesiastical Antiquities*, his very own diocesan handbook?

(v) Reeves materials now reprinted

Modern readers may also use the *Antiquities* as their handbook in the field. For it has been appropriate in this centenary year to continue the programme of reprinting begun in 1988 with Robert King's *The Old Church of Ballynascreen* (xiii + 148 pages). That work is still available at £5 (incl. p & p) from Graham

Mawhinney, Orr's Corner, Labby, Draperstown, Co. Londonderry, BT45 7BG. Now also available from the same address, in a limited numbered edition of 500 copies (xxiv + 436 pages), at an introductory price of £19.50 each (incl. p & p), is a blue cased reprint of the *Antiquities*. Copies of Reeves' paper, "On the Townland Distribution of Ireland" (21 pages), may still be procured for £1.50 (incl. p & p). Ballymena's ecclesiastical antiquary has not gone unremembered in 1992.

Ascona Series: 8

ECCLESIASTICAL ANTIQUITIES

OF

DOWN, CONNOR, AND DROMORE,

CONSISTING OF

A TAXATION OF THOSE DIOCESES,

COMPILED IN THE YEAR MCCCVI.;

WITH

NOTES AND ILLUSTRATIONS

BY

THE REV. WILLIAM REEVES, M.B., M.R.I.A.,

PERPETUAL CURATE OF KILCONRIOLA, IN THE DIOCESE OF CONNOR

Original edition:

DUBLIN

HODGES AND SMITH, GRAFTON-STREET,

BOOKSELLERS TO THE UNIVERSITY

MDCCCXLVII

Reprinted for the centenary of the author's death
with Biographical Introduction by Eull Dunlop

Braid Books & Moyola Books, 1992

65

Capella de Tener 1306 AD and Modern Tara in the Ards Peninsula

A.J. Hughes

In his monumental contribution to our understanding of the ecclesiastical history and archaeology of the area which roughly corresponds to modern counties Antrim and Down, the Rev. William Reeves presented us with a list of the churches of the dioceses of Down, Connor and Dromore featuring in the *Taxatio Ecclesiastica* of Pope Nicholas IV (*circa* 1306). Reeves then proceeded to synthesise references to these churches from available earlier Irish sources (such as martyrologies and annals), from contemporary medieval and later seventeenth century sources (such as registers, visitations, inquisitions, etc.), and from the modern forms of the placenames in question.[1] Despite the passage of practically one and a half centuries since its publication, Reeves' work remains a standard reference source, and the majority of its valuable findings have stood the test of time remarkably well. It is hardly surprising, however, that in a work of such magnitude certain peripheral details should remain to be sketched in and it is the purpose of the present note to refine somewhat the commentary on the *Capella de Tener* ('The Chapel of Tener [sic!]').

This entry appeared in the taxation in the portion dealing with the southern half of the Ards peninsula in Co. Down:

Ecclesia de Dere	(= Derry, td. in Ballyphilip parish)
Ecclesia de Feliptoñ	(= Ballyphilip parish)
Ecclesia de Thurstaynistoñ	(= Ballytrustan parish)
Vicaria eiusdem	(= vicarage of the same)
Capella de Tener	(= chapel of Tener)
Alba ecclesia	(= Whitechurch, par. Ballywalter)[2]

Having successfully identified the sites of the churches surrounding *Capella de Tener*, Reeves (p. 25, n. v) listed *Tener* as 'Now Witter, a parish at the extreme end of the Ards'. Witter is listed as a civil parish in the nineteenth-century six-inch OS survey of Ireland and similar sources.[3] John O'Donovan wrongly conjectured that the name *Witter* corresponded to an original Irish *lochtar* 'the lower part or extremity',[4] but Reeves, having the benefit of examining seventeenth century anglicised spellings along the lines of *Grange-oughter* goes back to an original Irish *Gráinseach Uachtair* 'Grange of

66

Uachtar', where *Uachtar* was the name of the area around Tara which survives as the parish *Witter*. *Uachtar* means 'upper, or high, region'.

It seems strange that Reeves did not comment on the modern form of the name *Capella de Tener* especially as he continues (p. 25 n. v) that "Close by the shore on Tara Bay, is the long-disused cemetery containing the faint outline of the foundations of a church, about fifty-four feet long, and eighteen feet broad. The spot is called 'Templecowey'." If this church is to be identified as representing an Irish-language *Teamapall Chú Mhaighe* 'Church of St. Cowey' then an identification of Cowey, or Cú Maighe ('Hound of the Plain'), will have to be conducted elsewhere, as the issue to be considered here is the identification and function of the medieval *Capella de Tener* and its subsequent appellation as modern *Witter*. The form *Tener* in the ecclesiastical taxation of Pope Nicholas IV represents a scribal error in the transmission of this name, as we might have expected *Tever*, or *Temer*. Our reason for expecting a spelling resembling the latter forms is based on the fact that the modern townland of Tara can be traced back to an earlier Irish *Teamhair*, pronounced as something resembling [t'ever'].

An Archaeological Survey of County Down, p. 173, contains a brief comment on and plan of Tara Fort, although there is no mention of the fact that this place featured in early Irish literature, as in the tale *Mesca Ulad* 'The Intoxication of the Ulstermen' – a tale forming part of the general corpus of the heroic literature known as the Ulster Cylcle and surviving in the twelfth-century Book of Leinster – there is mention of *Blad Briuga mac Fiachna a Temair na hArdda*,[7] i.e. 'Blad Briuga son of Fiachna from Temair [= modern Tara] of the Ards'. Blad Briuga 'Blad the Hospitaller' was one of the Ulster heroes, as E. O'Curry summarises, 'who, in a fit of excitement, after a great feast at the royal palace of Emania, made a furious march into Munster, where they burned the palace of *Teamhair Luachra* in Kerry, then residence of *Curoi Mac Dairé*, king of West Munster.'[8] While R. Hennessy tentatively suggested an identification between *Temair na hArda* and Tara ringfort in the Ards,[9] a view also expressed by E. Hogan,[10] further positive proof as to the veracity of this identification was provided by J. Carmichael Watson who pointed out that in the version of the tale *Mesca Ulad* contained in Gaelic MS XL in the National Library of Scotland the text read Teamuir Arda .i. *Ard Ulad*,[11] or 'Tara of (the) Ards, i.e. the Ards of Ulster.'

Thus, having safely identified *Teamhair* as the underlying Irish form for modern Tara in the Ards, we can see that the reference to *Capella de Tener* from 1306 is a reference to the ruined church at Tara, the ruins of which are not discussed in *An Archaeological Survey of County Down*, but which were described in broad outline by Reeves (*op. cit.*).

Tracing the shift from fourteenth century *Ecclesia de Tener* to seventeenth century *Grange-Oughter* has been greatly facilitated by a reference to this church in a document, dating to *circa* 1300 AD, which deals with Ulster lands in possession of St. Mary's Abbey Dublin,[12] where details are given of lands in *tenemento de Thewer in Ardis* (i.e. 'in the tenement of Thewer in the Ards'), among them:

> *Item:* **grangia de Thewer**, *in quo ii. carucata terre*
>
> i.e. 'Item: the grange of Thewer in which are two carucates of land'

The change of *capella* to *grangia* of Tara is hardly a surprising one, if one accepts Flanagan's view of this element:

"*gráinseach* (<Norman-French *grange*), 'grange, monastic farm' … frequently occurs in placenames without further qualification, commonly as Grange and sometimes in the anglicised form Gransha. It refers to a land-unit, generally a townland, held as a farm-land (or possibly simply grain-producing land) by a monastic house of the 12th or post-12th century period, frequently an Anglo-Norman foundation. The 'grange' need not necessarily adjoin the monastery; it might be some distance, removed from it. In the Lecale area of Co. Down the units of Grangicam (*Gráinseach Cham* 'crooked grange'), Grangewalls and Grangeban were the granges of one or other of the several monastic foundations in the Downpatrick area, and some distance removed from them. The term *grange* in some instances came to be used as the equivalent of parish, where a block unit or adjoining lands were held by the monastic house, as in the case of the Grange of Muckamore, Co. Antrim."[13]

In the case of *Witter*, Co. Down, we may add a further example of how the *grangia* could progress to assume parish status from the *capella*, doubtless due to the corn-producing activity in the area surrounding the Anglo-Norman *Capella de Thewer*. What remains is the fact that the name was gaelicised in the medieval period as *Gráinseach Uachtair* 'Grange of Uachtar', rather than **Gráinseach na Teamhrach*, which seemed to be a potential gaelicisation judging by the form *grangia de Thewer* in 1300 AD.[14] The fact that *Uachtair* was chosen as a qualifier rather than *na Teamhrach* may be explained by the fact that *Uachtar* designated 'of the upper part (of the Ards)' or modern Witter, i.e. that this grange was in the area known as the *Little Ards*, as opposed to the *Capella de Grangia* 'Chapel of Grangia', listed in the 1306 taxation of Nicholas IV[15] and which Reeves successfully identified as the modern townland of Gransha in the parish of Inishargy. Although both the parishes of Inishargy and Witter are nowadays in the barony of the Upper Ards, in the medieval period the former was in the *le Magna Arda* or *Great Ards*, while the latter was in the *Little Ards* and both of these would have been separated by water near the modern river Blackstaff, on the southern boundary of the modern townland of Gransha, and it is evident that, at the time when *Gráinseach Uachtair* was used for Witter in the Little Ards, the townland of Gransha in the Great Ards was qualified as by the prefix *Cúl–* 'Back–' thus in an inquisition taken as late as the reign of Charles I we read: *Coolegrane aliis Grange in le Great Ardes prope Blackstaff*[16] (1644 AD). This is equivalent to Irish *Cúl-Ghráinseach* 'back-grange'.

All things considered, then, one can see that whatever the association between the church ruins in the townland of Tara and a Saint *Cú Mhaighe*,[17] in the Anglo-Norman period there was an ecclesiastical establishment functioning here, albeit as a small concern judging by its low levy of 20*s* in the papal taxation of 1306,[18] and the change of *Capella de Tener* to *grangia de Thewer* (later still *Grange-oughter* > *Witter*) reflects, topographically, the importance attached to corn production in the Anglo-Norman church in the Ards, an importance touched upon by Flanagan (1982-4:75) for the nearby barony of Lecale, Co. Down.

Indeed, as regards the suitability of the Ards for the production of corn – a fact suggested by the number of medieval granges – we may note that in the later Elizabethan and post-Plantation periods references abound to its cultivation here. In a 'Tract by Sir Thomas Smith on the Colonisation of Ards in County Down' 1572 AD it is recommended that 'every Souldiour shal put his share towards the sowing and manuring thereof, and receive his parte of the corne and other profite that is to be gathered thereon, which we shall come to him besides his maintenance from the cuntrie."[19] Elsewhere in this tract (p. 411) it is proposed that 'there be one Hauen with common Granyers made upon the key, sufficient for the receipt of the Corne of the Cuntry' while on p. 412 it is urged that 'corne to be put in the ground against next yeare.'

In a letter from Sir Ralfe Lane to secretary Cecil dating to 1602, the Ards is described as 'a country of nine miles in length and five in breadth of the best corn ground in Ireland.'[20] In the late seventeenth century account of the barony of the Ards by William Montgomery in 1683 it is mentioned that: "This Barroney is divided in lower and vpper otherwise called ye little and great Ardes ye first whereof next Lacahill send euery winter great store of good Wheat beare oats and Barley to Dublin and els where."[21]

Notes

1. Reeves, W (ed.), *Ecclesiastical Antiquities of Down, Connor, and Dromore consisting of a taxation of those dioceses compiled in the year MCCCVI with notes and illustrations,* Dublin, 1847.

2. Details *ibid.* 22-7.

3. See, for example, the description of the parish of Witter in Day, A. & McWilliams, P. (eds.), *Ordnance Survey Memoirs of Ireland: Parishes of Down II 1832-4, 1837 North Down and the Ards,* Vol. 7, pp. 125-7 (Belfast, 1991); or in Lewis, S., *A Topographical Index of Ireland ...* Vol. II, pp. 723-4 (London, 1837).

4. *Ordnance Survey Name-Books, Co. Down* parish of Witter.

5. Reeves *ibid.* 25, n.v.

6. Hannan, R.J. & Hughes, A.J., *The Place-Names of the Ards Barony* (Co. Down Place-Names Vol. 2, Institute of Irish Studies, Queen's University Belfast) forthcoming.

7. Best, R.I. and O'Brien, M.A. (eds.), *The Book of Leinster* Vol. 5, (Dublin, 1967) p. 1184, I. 35088.

8. O'Curry, E., *Lectures on the manuscript materials of ancient Irish history,* (Dublin 1861) p. 185.

9. '*Temair-na-hArda,* now probably Tara, barony of Upper Ards, Co. Down', Hennessy, R. (ed.), '*Mesca Ulad* or the Intoxication of the Ultonians' *Todd Lecture Series* Vol. 1, part 1, p. v, n. 11 (Dublin, 1889).

10. *Onomasticon Goedelicum* (Dublin, 1910) p. 630.

11. Watson, J.C. (ed.), *Mesca Ulad,* Dublin Institute for Advanced Studies 1967, p. 129 (earlier p. 31, notes to line 715).

12. Gilbert, J.T. (ed.), *Chartularies of St. Mary's Abbey, Dublin,* Vol. 1 (Dublin, 1884) p. 4.

13. Flanagan, D., 'A summary guide to the more commonly attested ecclesiastical elements in place-names', *Bulletin of the Ulster Place-Names Society* ser. 2, vol. 4 (1981-2) pp. 69-75 (at p. 75).

14. Cf. for example anglicised spellings for the townland of Tara – such as *Ballyntawragh* (1571), *Ballenetauragh* (1927) – which are indicative of an Irish *Baile na Teamhrach* 'The townland of Tara'.

15. Reeves, *op. cit.* 21, n. m.

16. Details in Reeves, *op. cit.*

17. No mention is made of a *Cú M(h)aig(h)e* in Ó Riain, P. (ed.), *Corpus genealogiarum Sanctorum Hiberniae,* (Dublin, 1985).

18. Cf., However, the Pipe Roll for the regnal year XI Edward III for apparently significant commercial trading brought about by the herring fishery 'in the tenement of *Teuere* [= Tara] near the shore in the county of Ulster' (Appendix to *39th Report of the Deputy Keeper of the Public Records of Ireland,* p. 23).

19.   Cited in pp. 405-15 of Hill, G., *An Historical Account of the MacDonnells of Antrim*, (Belfast, 1837) at p. 408.

20.   Mahaffy, Robert Pentland (ed.), *Calendar of the State Papers relating to Ireland 1601-3*, PRO London, 1912, p. 315).

21.   Quinn, D.B. (ed.), 'William Montgomery and the description of the Ards, 1683', *Irish Booklore*, vol. 2, no. 1 (1972) 29-43 (at p. 34).

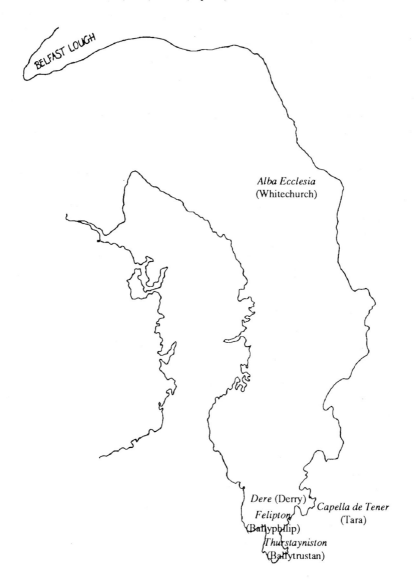

Ordnance Survey Maps in the Public Record Office of Northern Ireland

T.J. Parkhill

The Public Record Office of Northern Ireland (PRONI) has a large and comprehensive collection of maps on various scales produced by the Ordnance Survey (OS) since its establishment in the early 1830s. The most recent estimate accounts for over forty thousand printed and manuscript OS maps, from a total number of fifty-five thousand maps (figures which in themselves give an idea of the scale of PRONI's holdings).[1] As a result, PRONI can claim to serve the research interests of every area in Northern Ireland, no matter how small, since every foot of ground is represented on a map. Moreover, it is possible to trace the development of any local area by comparing early editions with later versions. For the local historian interested in a rural area, the best scale to consult is the County series on the scale of six inches to one statute mile (1:10560).[2] The townland maps on this scale for the whole of Ireland were completed by 1842. It is one of their many benefits as a source for pre-Famine Ireland that the mapping was carried out when the country had its maximum recorded population.[3]

There were three subsequent editions of the six-inch OS maps. For Ulster the principal dates are 1853-61 for the publication of the second edition; 1903-06 for the third edition; and 1921-39 for the fourth edition; all are on the scale of six-inches to one mile.[4] And, because they are on the same scale, the respective editions can also be compared and an evaluation undertaken of what has changed and what has remained the same in any local area. The importance of the idea of 'continuity and change' in our environment has been recognised in a number of ways, not least by the Department of Education (NI), by the Community Relations Council and by the many voluntary bodies (prominent among which is the Federation for Ulster Local Studies) who seek to broaden our understanding of the two main traditions in Northern Ireland. At a practical level, the maps of the OS enable a study of developments in a local area over the last one hundred and fifty years, effectively five generations, to be discovered.

On the six-inch scale, the number of sheets required to ensure the full coverage of each county ranges from thirty for Co. Armagh to seventy-one for Co. Tyrone. Each sheet covers twenty-four square miles of countryside and the availability of the four editions enables studies to be undertaken on patterns of settlement, on transport (including roads, canals and railways) and on local industries, particularly linen. Field and natural boundaries, mineral resource sites such as quarries and individual features of the local landscape can be traced and identified, and any changes that might have affected them since the 1830s can be noted. The extent of local detail that was recorded did vary from area to area and from surveyor to surveyor. It cannot therefore be assumed that, because 'Peter Bryant's bullock hole' is recorded in the townland of Greenan on sheet 37 of Co. Fermanagh, every idiosyncratic local feature will be so recorded (though it is interesting to know that it appears on the subsequent second and third editions of 1859 and 1903). The maps are, otherwise, a faithful record of the landscape in the 1830s. Man-made items and settlement features such as roads, big houses, churches of all denominations, police barracks, post offices and schools are recorded. And the nineteenth-century interest in antiquities was reflected in the care taken to mark castles, ancient ruins, early Christian and mediaeval churches as well as archaeological sites.

Ordnance Survey maps on the six-inch scale are particularly valuable for plotting the location of the hundreds of flax and corn mills that were dotted throughout the Ulster countryside in the nineteenth century. It is always worth remembering that, before mechanical power was available for manufacturing purposes, the reliance on water for power meant that the countryside was more industrialised than towns: factories needed to be beside water with a natural or artificial flow which turned the wheels of industry. The OS maps remain the best means of representing this concept. Few sheets will not have a mill recorded on them; many will have several and there are instances, particularly in counties Down and Tyrone, where some ten or twelve mills might be found on the one sheet covering twenty-four square miles.[5]

The potential of the maps for a study of the industrial archaeology of a locale is exemplified in *The Industrial Archaeology of Northern Ireland*[6] which uses not only OS maps but also the valuation maps of the 1830s (which were really OS maps on which the valuers identified buildings and lands to be valued) and, more particularly, the valuers' field books in which are recorded working details of mills such as the months of the year in which they normally operated, the size of wheel and whether it is breastshot, undershot or overshot.[7] There remains today evidence of those buildings, machinery and equipment on the original sites and more than one local historical society has organised a field trip to examine the evidence of flax, corn and, in the case of Randalstown, printing mills and have supplemented their site visit by research in libraries, particularly using newspapers, and in the PRO.

In at least three other respects which are of general interest to local historians – archaeological sites, placenames, and schools before the National System of Education – the first edition OS maps have served as a valuable historical record in their own right. The survey was the first reliable and methodical registering of sites of antiquity which are in themselves evidence of Ireland in early times. J.H. Andrews points out that 'many antiquities were noticed on the plans; a few were not sketched or separately mapped',[8] many of the sketches also featuring in the Ordnance Survey Memoirs. Mistakes in identification and classification of sites were made, but Andrews' view is that although 'there are some expressions such as druid's altar and giant's grave (for megalithic tombs) which have been scorned by later archaeologists ... the Survey could be defended by classing these as names rather than descriptions'.[9]

The role of the Survey in recording and standardising townland names is a service for which not only local historians but students of the Irish language, geographers and folklorists should be grateful. 'Placenames', said Andrews, 'are among the best documented features of the six-inch map',[10] though it should be noted that although the final survey was completed by 1846, no index of townland names appeared until 1862.[11] Much of the credit for recording both placenames and antiquities must, of course, be attributed to John O'Donovan and also, it should be said, to Thomas Larcom for allowing O'Donovan the freedom to indulge his interests and great learning.

The registering of schools on maps which were compiled in the early 1830s is an effective means of demonstrating how many places of education had been established before the national system came into effect. The number per sheet obviously varies but, for example, one sheet for the Rathfriland district of Co. Down records no less than ten schools in 1833.[12] This bears out the findings of the Report of Inquiry into Education 1826-27 which showed that Ulster in general and Co. Down in particular had the highest ratio of schools for pupils in Ireland and, using that criterion at least, Down had the best provision for education (in the English language) in Ireland.[13]

In addition to the six-inch maps, the first survey produced other records, the most significant of which are undoubtedly the Memoirs. It is far beyond the scope of this article to do anything other than mention them. There are, however, other manuscript records made by the Ordnance officers at the time of the original survey which have survived and which should be drawn to researchers' interest more often than they have been. Among these sources are the Boundary Registers[14] which record the measurements, directions and observations of the Royal Engineers who charted the boundaries between townlands. An example taken at random may illustrate how these volumes, when used with the first edition six-inch maps, can recreate a detailed picture of the countryside as it must have been in the 1830s:

> "Terrydremont North, from its function with Edenmore and Drumachose the mereing takes the right ditch of a lane running from the Bog ... crossing the road from Newtown Limavady to Dungiven immediately after which a small stream becomes the mereing passing a smith's shop about 1 chain to the right, keeping a north-west course for 5 chains and ... falls into the River Roe the centre of which becomes the mereing dividing the Parishes of Tamlaght Finlagan and Balteagh. The mereing ... leaves the river ... and passing within 40 links of a Flax Mill to the right and 1 chain to the left of a cabin where it meets a lane which it crosses diagonally..."[15]

The possibility of re-tracing the map-makers' perambulations can be realised using this source, in association with the maps of the first edition of the Survey. The painstaking care in delineating the boundaries of townlands and parishes that is evident in the Boundary registers is sufficient to give credence to the claim that the first edition maps are the accurate and official arbiters in deciding where townlands and parishes start and finish. As Andrews points out, 'legally, the boundaries of the ordnance map, unlike those the Downe Survey, are entirely devoid of proprietorial significance',[16] and that when the first edition was revised, the first county to be surveyed, Londonderry, saw no fewer than 1654 of its townlands have their boundaries altered. It can be claimed, however, that the publication of the Ordnance Survey maps had the general effect of stabilising the townland pattern of Ireland.

The second edition of the six-inch scale was begun in Co. Londonderry in the late 1840s, and most of the Ulster county maps were published between 1852 and 1863. One of the most striking innovations on the landscape that is recorded on the second edition of the Survey maps is, of course, the railway. The labyrinthine networking, achieved in a very short time between the ending of the first edition in the early 1840s and the second edition (in Ulster) of the later 1850s and early 1860s, is immediately noticeable when comparing any first and second edition map: few second edition sheets are without railway lines. The introduction of workhouses, national schools, more roads and bridges are all representative of 'change' in the mid-nineteenth century. And the impression of change is emphasised all the more by the recording of field boundaries on the second and subsequent editions. This feature was not included on the original maps, mainly because the valuation of the 1830s was

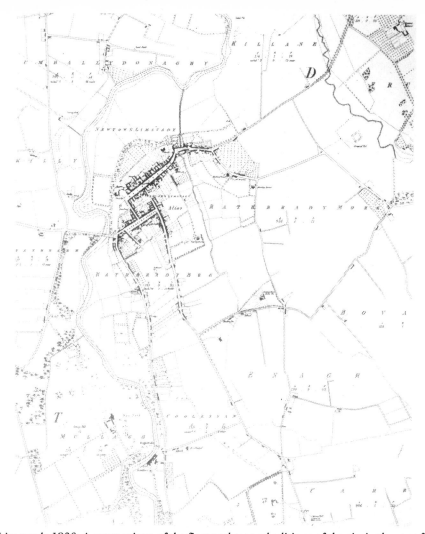

Limavady 1830. A comparison of the first and second editions of the six-inch maps for Limavady (above) shows the development of a provincial town in the mid-nineteenth century. The railway, which is first recorded in the second edition, would appear to have acted as a stimulus to and a focus for industrial growth.

to be an assessment of each townland, rather than individual properties or fields, for the payment of rates. The first edition looks, in consequence, to have a rather bare, incomplete appearance, and when they are overlaid, for comparative purposes, with the second edition, the inclusion of the field boundaries creates a striking sense of change.

Limavady 1848-52. A corn mill, a gas works, a weaving factory and a brewery are situated close to the railway station. There are also more schools and markets on the 1848-52 sheet. The sense of rapid change is emphasised by the introduction of field boundaries, which are not included on the first edition maps. PRONI OS 6/5/9/1 and 2.

Nevertheless, a closer study of the four editions between 1830s and 1930s will yield evidence of the continuity that links one generation with the next. The location of churches, houses, road patterns, rivers, mill races (which are still recorded even if, by the time of the later editions, they are no longer in use), archaeological sites (a number of which are recorded on some but not all editions) and other antiquities all represent elements of constancy even in a society which is modernising rapidly. The pace and nature of the developments in nineteenth-century society, particularly in towns in Ulster, may be seen by comparing the first and second edition of the six-inch sheets on which provincial towns are found. The town of Limavady, seen here on the first and second edition OS six-inch maps (dated 1830 and 1848-52 respectively),[17] has not only expanded in size but shows all the signs of having a more industrial base and the provision of greater services for a growing population. The railway had arrived and appears to have acted as a stimulus to and focus for industry. Gas was being produced locally, a corn mill, a weaving factory and a brewery were all in close proximity, a workhouse had been built and several schools and more markets were to be found in the town.

The third and fourth editions, published for Ulster counties c.1901-06 and 1919-39 respectively, contain details of further additions and changes. 'It was their facility for receiving further information that made the six-inch maps so useful to scientists and scholars', observes Andrews, on the value of editions which succeeded the primary survey. His view is that 'the new [revised] maps have never rivalled the old ones in public favour. For the modern student ... the later [eighteen] forties and the fifties lack the obvious historical interest of the pre-famine period.'[18] And there is no doubt that there is almost an emotional association of the first edition maps with the 'lost' period of pre-famine Ireland. However, this must not eclipse the importance of the subsequent editions which, because they bring up-to-date the developments in the countryside since the 1830s, are an irreplaceable record of continuity and change.

Local historical interest should, at this stage, be referred to a new scale which the Ordnance Survey introduced in the 1890s, the twenty-five inch scale. This was obviously on a larger scale than the six-inch maps; in fact, it takes sixteen sheets on the twenty-five inch (1:2500) scale to cover the same area of one sheet on the six-inch scale. Although official approval of a larger scale for rural areas (urban areas were already being mapped on larger scales) was granted, for outskirts of Derry city, in 1869 and the map published in 1873, it was not until the turn of the century that a completed survey of the Ulster counties was available on the scale of 1:2500. There were two main series published in the first quarter of the twentieth century: the first edition between 1894 and 1904 and the second edition between 1920-1924. A significant number of the sheets on this scale were published again in the early 1930s and some fewer sheets re-published in the early 1950s. The general series in which these maps are held in PRONI is known as the '25-inch county series'.[19] As may be imagined from their enlarged scale, they are particularly useful for delineating the physical shapes of buildings and houses including even their out-buildings; they can also be used to locate milestones, post office boxes, water pumps and the 'street furniture' of Victorian and Edwardian society. They also record detail of hedgerows, road verges, gardens etc. that are not apparent in the six-inch maps, so they have an environmental as well as historical interest.

The twenty-five inch County series was undertaken when the full benefits of the large-scale mapping of towns first became apparent, in the 1850s and 1860s. There had been large-scale mappings of towns prior to that: the earliest known is of Derry city, dated 1827 with revisions in 1831.[20] It was understood from the outset of the Ordnance Survey that the valuation of towns, for which purpose the maps were being made, would require larger-scale maps than that of rural areas. Between the first operations of the Survey in Ireland in 1825 and the beginning of the valuation in 1830, there was no firm policy as to which towns should be mapped or the scale of the town maps. From 1833, some one hundred towns in the island were mapped on the scale of five feet to one mile (1:1056). The PRONI has copies of the maps which were published for 163 towns in the province of Ulster, and manuscript maps for some fifty towns, many in several editions. They form part of an important section of the Ordnance Survey archive held in PRONI: in all, there are town plans for over one hundred and ninety towns described in the two main catalogues. OS 8 has the published maps of the one hundred and sixty three urban settlements; OS 9 contains manuscript maps for some fifty towns, twenty-four of which are on the scale of 1:500 (ten feet to one mile).

The Towns Improvement Act of 1854 empowered towns to provide themselves with five-foot plans of the areas under their jurisdiction and in 1857 the Survey took the decision to make plans for all Irish towns on the scale of 1:500, ten feet to one mile. The Valuation Office, however, complained that this was too large a scale, and certainly many of the larger towns required up to twenty sheets when this scale was used. For example, there are fifteen sheets of manuscript plans for Bangor on the scale of 1:500 in 1859, and six sheets on the scale of 1:1056 in 1895-96; eleven sheets for Banbridge on the 1:500 scale in 1861 and again in 1889-92; for Londonderry on the 1:500 scale in 1873 there are thirty-four sheets; for Armagh, twenty-four sheets in 1862 on the scale of 1:500; for Lisburn twelve sheets on the 1:500 scale in 1861 ad 1876.

The maps of twenty-four Ulster towns – Tandragee, Rathfriland, Portaferry, Newtownhamilton, Newtownards, Newry, Markethill, Lisburn, Londonderry,

Killyleagh, Kilkeel, Keady, Hillsborough, Gilford, Dromore (Co. Down), Downpatrick, Donaghadee, Comber, Coleraine, Bangor, Banbridge, Armagh, Ballynahinch, Ardglass – on the scale of 1:500 were published c. 1861 and are a very detailed record of those towns in the middle of the nineteenth century. They were subsequently used for valuation purposes.

After the early 1860s, the predominant scale on which towns were mapped was 1:1056. The majority of the published town plans held in PRONI are on this scale and date from the 1870s or 1880s, or for the early years of the twentieth century, 1902-05. From the point of view of local history research, the widespread availability of maps on this scale is very helpful. The scale is not too unwieldly and only the largest towns occupy more than two or three sheets; the majority are to be found on one sheet. They make a good foundation on which a study of a town or village can be undertaken. It could become a future trivial pursuit question, but if anyone is ever asked the question 'How many towns are there in Ulster?', one way of answering is to reply 'Well, there are plans for one hundred and ninety-two urban settlements in Ulster which are held in PRONI'. They range from conurbations as large as Belfast, Londonderry, Armagh and Newry to modest centres such as Stranocum, Mosside and Templepatrick in Co. Antrim, Mountnorris, Laurel Vale and Acton in Co. Armagh, Shrigley, Scarva and Seaforde in Co. Down, Ballinamallard, Tempo and Maguiresbridge in Co. Fermanagh, Swatragh, Feeny and Garvagh in Co. Londonderry and Termon Rock, Fintona and Fivemiletown in Co. Tyrone.[21]

For the more recent period, the availability of the Irish Grid six-inch series and twenty-five inch series should be brought to the local historian's attention. The six-inch Irish Grid survey was begun in the early years of the present century, and the maps for the Ulster counties began to be published at the end of the Great War. As a consequence, much of this series overlaps with the six-inch County series. The Irish Grid six-inch series in OS 7, on the scale of 1:10560, covers the years 1919-1960s. The twenty-five inch Irish Grid survey was developed considerably later and the first maps published for Northern Ireland in 1954. They are also included in the OS 11 series in PRONI which continues until the mid-1970s.

This article has concentrated on the main series of OS maps which are available for Ulster local historical research: the six-inch County series; the twenty-five inch County series; large-scale town plans; and the Irish Grid series in both six-inch and twenty-five inch scales. There are other sections of the Ordnance Survey archive whose value would be evident on a visit to PRONI. For example, OS 32 contains a series of townland index maps which should help demographers, geographers and local historians as much as they have served genealogists searching on their own or their clients' behalf. The concentration on the main six-inch, twenty-five inch and sixty-inch series should, however, give an idea of the use to which they can be put, and an assurance that, no matter where the area you are interested in is located, it will be described on Ordnance Survey maps going back to the 1830s. Few pieces of local historical research, for rural or urban areas, will not benefit from a close scrutiny of Ordnance Survey maps which are available (and which can be copied at a modest charge) in the Public Record Office of Northern Ireland.

Notes

1. *World Directory of Map Collections*, 3rd edition (forthcoming). To be published by McGill University Press, Montreal.

2. PRONI OS 1. The maps are arranged alphabetically by county: Co. Antrim is OS 1/1, Co. Armagh OS 1/2 and so on. The researcher can find the appropriate sheet on which his local area of interest is located by referring to the Topographical Index available in PRONI and in libraries. For example, Rathfriland, Co. Down is on sheet 41. So the reference will be OS 1/3/41.

3. The population of Ireland was 7,767,401 in 1831 and 8,175,124 in 1841. See Report of the Commissioners appointed to take the Census of Ireland, 1841. HC 1843 [504] XXIV.

4. The various editions are available in OS 6 in PRONI. They are arranged on the same basis as described in footnote 2.

5. See, for example, OS 6/3/41/2, on which eleven flax and corn mills are sited.

6. W.A. McCutcheon, *The Industrial Archaeology of Northern Ireland*, HMSO, 1980.

7. See the valuers' field books in the series in PRONI, VAL.1B.

8. J.H. Andrews, *A Paper Landscape*, p. 177. OUP. 1975.

9. *Ibid.*, pp. 128-9.

10. *Ibid.*, p. 126.

11. *General Alphabetical Index to the townlands, towns, parishes and baronies of Ireland ...* Dublin, 1861. Reprinted (1984) by the Genealogical Publishing Co. Inc., Baltimore, Maryland, USA.

12. PRONI OS 1/3/41.

13. 2nd Report of the Commission of Inquiry into Irish Education. HC 1826-7, XII.

14. PRONI, OS 4.

15. *Loc. cit.*, OS 4/5B/13A.

16. Andrews, *op. cit.*, p. 141.

17. PRONI OS 6/5/9/1 and OS 6/5/9/2.

18. Andrews, *op. cit.*, p. 141.

19. PRONI OS 10 contains the first and second editions on the twenty-five inch scale. They are arranged similarly to the OS 1 and OS 6 series, alphabetically by county. A grid map is available in the Public Search Room to guide the reader to the appropriate sheets.

20. Andrews, *op. cit.*, p. 228.

21. *Northern Ireland Town Plans 1828-1966: a catalogue of large scale town plans prepared by the Ordnance Survey and deposited in PRONI*, pub. by PRONI 1981. Available on request from the Public Search Room, £1 (allow 50p for postage if requesting by post).

A Tribute to No Ordinary Woman
Miss Mabel Remington Colhoun

K. Gormley

My first meeting with Miss Mabel Colhoun was in January 1987 when I first attended the monthly meeting of the North West Archaeological and Historical Society in Magee College. She was at that stage past President of the Society but remained a prominent, much respected and well loved committee member until her death on 4th April 1992.

During this time we were privileged to hear many of her memories and listen to talks and tours given by her. Among her lat was an illustrated lecture on the archaeology of Inishowen given to the Society and the Londonderry Naturalists' Field Club in November 1991 and on Archaeology day 1988 the NWAHS and friends were treated to a tour of Inishowen by Mabel.

Part of the day included a visit to Culdaff House which Mabel's father had rebuilt in the 1920s. She was presented with a crystal bowl in recognition of her contribution to local history and to the NWAHS by Mr. Charles Logue, President of the Society.

However, recognition of Mabel went far beyond the boundaries of our Society. She was a former President of the Londonderry Naturalists' Field Club, a Vice-President and Fellow of the Royal Society of Antiquaries of Ireland and a committee member of the Donegal Historical Society. She was among those in the latter society who took the initiative in asking all similar societies to examine the possibility of grouping together for mutual aid and interest, at a meeting in Ballybofey in 1974. Hence the Federation for Ulster Local Studies was born.

Mabel was an organiser by nature and a person with great foresight. In her earlier years she had trained at the National Froebel Union, had taught at

Bournemouth, set up her own private school in Derry and eventually became Head of the Preparatory part of the High School whose aim it was "to send out into the world girls who are useful and happy in home and professional life." As Principal she was renowned for always getting 'to the bottom of things.'

Mabel's particular interest was in the history and archaeology of Inishowen. This was fostered by her uncle, Charles Gordon, the historian. She was further encouraged in this field by Oliver Davies who invited

Mabel describing the slab cross at Fahan Abbey on Archaeology Day, September 1988.

her to join him on an archaeological dig. Mabel bought her first pair of trousers for this excursion. Her reputation for detail and knowledge became known far and wide and she was asked to contribute her knowledge and photographs (of which she had a huge collection) to Harry Swan's books on Inishowen. In 1940 she was invited by Professor Evans to come on a field trip to Ballyarnet with a group of students from Queen's University. She was at this stage persuaded to start recording archaeological sites in Inishowen. Much of her later life was devoted to a detailed survey of archaeology of this area. Mabel's sharp eye and ability to get local people to talk about their locality made her survey compulsive reading.

Presentation to Mabel in Culdaff House

Her work on this survey was started by bicycle in the 1930's and was continued by car until the late 70's, when an attempt to publish it proved unsuccessful. She was very pleased when the society agreed to back the undertaking only a short time before she died. The same determination to see her book was still there when I last saw Mabel in hospital a few days before she died. Her work is now in the hands of the Society and Annesley Malley has been working extensively on revising maps, etc. We are seeking funding to publish this work as Mabel wished. In her honour the North West Archaeological and Historical Society will hold a Memorial Lecture on Thursday, 18th February 1993 in Central Library.

Mabel, during her long life which has spanned every decade of this century, has done a great service to local history. She once referred in an article to one of the Federation's Past Presidents as 'an outstanding person full of knowledge and interest'; I am sure he, and all of us, would say the same of Mabel.

Reviews

Carrothers, D.S. (comp.), *Memoirs of a Young Lieutenant: 1898-1917*, 90pp. p/back.

Memoirs of a Young Lieutenant contains a personal account of a telling part of the life history of John Samuel Carrothers (a youngest son, born near Tamlaght, Co. Fermanagh, in 1898) between the summers of 1914 and 1917. This volume consists of fifty-three letters and postcards (exact copies) written by John Carrothers from his various postings: London, Dublin, Berkhamsted in Herts., Fermoy in Cork, Londonderry, Southampton and France; and they provide us with a one-way reconstruction of the journey between 'joining-up' and being lost in action – 'one way' because, unfortunately, no copies of correspondence received from home presumably now exist.

John Carrothers joined the British Army in 1915, having been employed by the Irish Land Commission Office in Dublin, and was accepted by the Officers' Training Corps (OTC) in December of that year. He received his commission as a 2nd Lieutenant with the 3rd Battalion, Royal Inniskilling Fusiliers in December, 1916, and was posted to France in January the following year. Most of the letters included in this volume were penned in France, his last known letter being dated 16th August, 1917. By this stage, John Carrothers was already a veteran.

However, some of his more interesting letters were written during his postings to London and Dublin during 1916. In a letter from the Inns of Court OTC, London, dated 1st January, 1916, he candidly describes popular anticipation of a 'Zepp. raid' on the capital, and goes on to comment on the news that 'conscription is not to apply to Ireland.' In a letter dated shortly afterwards, he refers to the composition of his 'squad' as being half Irish and half English, with the 'North and South of Ireland chaps' quarrelling over which songs to sing on their route march, and the locals being greatly amused by the 'wild Irishmen!' On a more sombre note, he points out that there are 'as many slackers here as in Dublin, and that says a good deal.'

He arrived in Dublin on 24th April, instantly finding the streets to be 'most unhealthy on account of "Sinn Fein" snipers and stray bullets.' His new posting was to a city caught up in the middle of national turmoil and political upheaval: indeed, in his letter to his mother, he warns her that it may in fact be censored before leaving the barracks. The insights to the minutiae of daily life and existence in Dublin during April of 1916 are both poignant and to the point.

However, they are much more than that; they are novel because they constitute a snap-shot of a city trying to come to terms with the aftermath of the Uprising from the viewpoint of a young Irishman in the British Army, Fermanagh born and bred, Unionist in upbringing and anti-Sinn Fein in principle.

What John Carrothers has to say on the events then unfolding all around him, we would do well to learn today: '...it is a fearful thing to fire even a rifle in the City, let alone machine guns or artillery.' Some are eye-witness accounts, others are the product of military life and internal channels of communication: Kingstown has been 'nearly levelled', officers of the Citizen Army have been marched in as prisoners 'just as dirty and hungry as ourselves', the 'S.F's in Jacobs have refused to surrender,' and have instead '...hoisted the flag of the Irish Republic', the 'Russian Countess who led this rebellion was brought in here as a prisoner', the great marble staircases of Dublin Castle are 'torn with bullets', and 'Sackville St., [now O'Connell Street] is half demolished by artillery ... a great pity ... as it is one of the finest streets in the world.' It is worth considering the following account, an account which was evanescent even at the time, finally and swiftly bowing to popular antipathy at the execution of the leaders of the Uprising:

"The citizens here all favour the military. It is pitiable to see some of the Sinns that have been captured by women in the back streets. They are all scratched and stabbed with hat-pins. Dublin is certainly ruined. No Irish men need look for a job in England now as we are considered worse than the Germans by the troops over from England and Wales."

After training in both England and Ireland, John Carrothers was eventually posted to France in February, 1917; now an officer in the British Expeditionary Force (BEF). At the outset he found it to be a 'splendid life' and had 'never been so glad' that he'd joined the Army before: this sentiment would not last long! His platoon thrived on the rum ration, got four ounces of tobacco a week, with cigarettes and matches making up the remainder. In the midst of trench warfare he could still hazard a guess that there would not be 'any trouble in giving the Huns the finishing touch this summer', and that after the trenches he would set his sights on 'some branch of the Regular Army', with 'The Indian Army' being the best. He took part in Wytschaete Ridge, a bloody battle full of fierce fighting, and wrote his mother that 'The Irish troops did the best of all and especially the Irish Brigade.' Of the prisoners they took, 'nearly every one of them was wearing the famous Iron Cross.' These were the best, 'Bavarians with a slight mixture of Prussian Guards and Death's Head Huzzars.' No longer did walking through 'hundreds of mangled corpses' unduly concern him.

In a letter to his mother from BEF dated 16th June, 1917, he informs her that Major Wm. Redmond (brother of John Redmond, then leader of the Irish Nationalist Party) had fallen beside him. He goes on to recount how a sergeant beside him looked up and said, 'It's a sorry day for Ireland Sir.' Major Redmond was hit by two bullets whilst taking part in the first wave of the attack, and was finally laid to rest in a little village that used to act as base for John Carrothers and his men. Redmond was a staff officer, not a line officer, and was felt by those around him to be inexperienced in the art of 'dodging shells'. A few days before sending his last known letter, John Carrothers summed up life in the trenches near Ypres as follows:

"My dug-out is dry but of course the door looks out the wrong way and is liable to catch any low fire from the Hun. We had a Capt. and several men sniped yesterday. A Lieutenant from another Coy. was hit yesterday morning too. I managed to get him to my dug-out. He groaned and bled all day so I had a time with him. He really only got a nice Blighty one which will ensure him not coming back to the war … Ypres or Wipers is a sight for the Gods. It stinks with poison gas and bad smells."

The last known letter from John Carrothers was, appropriately, to his mother, and is dated BEF, 13th August, 1917. Three days later, in his twentieth year, he was killed in action at Passchendaele and was listed as missing. A Lieutenant S.J. Henderson of the 3rd Royal Inniskilling Fusiliers wrote to the family on 25th February 1918, informing them that '…I heard he was badly wounded in the front line which he left on a stretcher borne by two bearers. After proceeding a short distance it is feared a shell got the whole party.' That is all we know. Memorial tablets have been placed in both Lisbellaw Presbyterian Church, Co. Fermanagh and Adelaide Road Presbyterian Church, Dublin.

This is an enlightening volume, containing the experiences and the expectations of a young officer, still in his teens and already a leader of men, who 'signed up' to fight for what he thought was right. It is a fascinating insight to the life led by such men: the constant preoccupation with the need to have good socks (a priority in the trenches), the refrain that he wasn't allowed to have a camera in the front line, learning life's lesson that there is a 'big difference between the weight of a rifle and a pen', commenting upon the 'weak voiced English chaps', castigating the loneliness of London, and all the time worrying about how things are at home on the land. These are the thoughts of an educated officer which have survived down through the years within the family, a first-hand and close-quarter's account of military life and martial rigour; short, sharp, clear and to the point. In the form of letters and postcards, they stand on their own; there is no narrative, no voice juxtaposed between John Carrothers and the reader, one of the most refreshing and endearing qualities of the volume.

Several full- and half-pages are devoted to postcard-covers and photographs, there are copies of plaques and badges, and the inside back-cover contains an estimate for an officer's uniform from McGee & Co. Ltd. of 2 Donegall Square West, Belfast, dated December, 1916, with an infantry great coat at 105 shillings and spiral putties at 8s. 6d. per pair – 'Officers' uniforms made to measure in 24 hours.'

Peter McNamee

Durnin, Patrick, *Derry and the Irish Poor Law, a history of the Derry Workhouse*, (The Waterside Community Local History Group, 1991). £4.50

Mr. Durnin has obviously put a lot of work into researching and writing what is a well-produced illustrated history of the Derry Workhouse. While one must voice some criticisms of the book, they are mainly of a technical nature – with regard to the footnotes, a list of abbreviations or giving the full title of the source on first entry would have helped, and in the text itself there is an over use of inverted commas. The language of the book is on the whole judgemental, or value-loaded, but when dealing with such a subject, particularly during the Great Famine, it is difficult to be otherwise.

However, Mr. Durnin does steer an unwavering course through the history of poor relief from earliest times to the introduction of the National Health Service in 1948. He gives us the background to society, politics and poverty in Derry in the early nineteenth century and the voluntary efforts to relieve the poor such as the Loan Fund and the Flax Fund. Usefully, too, he tells us of the growth of the city and the impact which the influx of large numbers of mainly Catholic rural poor had.

On the Irish Poor Relief Act itself, Mr. Durnin informs us of the thinking behind the Act and painstakingly follows its course through Parliament – including Daniel O'Connell's opposition – to its becoming law in 1838. The same regard for detail is given to his account of the implementation of the Act in Derry. In March of 1839 the first Derry Poor Law Guardians were assembled, and it is interesting to note that there was dispute over the election of their clerk. The Workhouse in the city was built on a design submitted by Wilkinson, the architect to the Poor Law Commissioners. Durnin is good on the staffing and running of the Workhouse, in particular on the philosophy underlying it all, such as the directive that "work should be of such a nature as to be irksome and to awaken or increase a dislike to remain in the Workhouse."

The whole system was put under intolerable strain by the Great Famine, leading to overcrowding, shortages of food and deaths caused by the consequent out-break of diseases. Overall it is quite a grim account of life, for both inmates and staff, during this period.

Mr. Durnin completes the story from the Famine on, outlining in detail the Vice-Regal Commission into the system of Poor Relief, the increasing criticism of it during this century and its eventual demise following the introduction of the National Health Service. While most readers'attention would be focussed on the era of the Great Famine, this section is also worth reading, giving as it does an account of society and attitudes to poverty and ill-health in more recent times.

All in all Mr. Durnin's book is to be commended. The Workhouse and the Great Famine figure largely in the folk memory of people all over Ireland. We all have an idea of what they were both like, so it is welcome to have an account firmly based in the use of primary sources and a judicious utilization of secondary works. While many may be surprised at the reality of the Workhouse system, readers of this book will come to understand why the Workhouse holds the position it does in the popular imagination.

Tony Canavan

Emery, James A., *The Passing Years of a Country Lodge, Garvetagh True Blues (Co. Tyrone) LOL 1486*, (Garvetagh True Blues, LOL 1486, 1990)

Centenary Booklet 1891-1991 Castlederg District Royal Black Chapter No. 6, (Castlederg District Royal Black Chapter No. 6, 1991)

Despite its long history and high public profile the nature and organisation of the Orange Order, and also the Royal Black Institution, remain something of a mystery to those outside these organisations. These two booklets, both from the Castlederg region, should enlighten anyone on the traditions and modern day workings of them. The first is a history of the Garvetagh True Blues by James A. Emery in which the author traces the Orange Order from its origins in "the earlier struggles of the 'Protestant Colony'" up to the present.

He gives a detailed account of the founding of the lodge in 1823, highlighting events in its own history, and also those of national significance in which it was involved such as the "Battle of Dromore" in 1884 when, along with other lodges, the Garvetagh True Blues travelled to that town "to support the landlords against the Nationalist tenant farmers" who were holding a Land League meeting. In the subsequent disturbances two Orangemen were injured, one named Griffin later dying of his wounds. Mr. Emery charts a course with a steady hand through the subsequent vicissitudes and triumphs of the lodge in the intervening decades to the present, recounting its history, and office holders; giving a good description of banners used through the years and the fortunes of its members.

The second booklet on the Castlederg District Royal Black Chapter brings us into a seemingly anachronistic and archane world of Sir Knights, pursuivants, preceptories and encampments with names like the Castlederg Chosen Few, Kerlish Golden Lights and the Garvetagh Guiding Star. This production is a detailed chronology of the history and personnel of this chapter from its foundation in 1891 to 1991. It also has a good account of the banners commissioned over the years and of this district's involvement in the major events such as the "Monster Demonstration of the Royal Black Institution in Omagh" on the 12th August 1924.

Both these books provide an insight not often granted to outsiders of the traditions of the Orange Order in Northern Ireland and the "Orange" perspective on our history as well as on more recent events. They highlight too the close knit harmony of the Protestant community, showing not only a cross-over between these two bodies but also how members of the Orange Order served with the Security Forces from the Ulster Special Constabulary to the U.D.R. and played their part in Unionist politics. Indeed both books are peppered with notices of the deaths of members who died while on duty with the Security Forces. For anyone genuinely concerned with Cultural Traditions who wishes to explore the diverse cultural heritage of Northern Ireland, then these booklets are an important contribution to the understanding of the Protestant traditions.

Tony Canavan

Field Boundaries 1-7, (Department of Agriculture for Northern Ireland, 1992).

Although aimed at the farmer, this series of leaflets will be of interest to any country dweller and in particular the local historian. The seven booklets look at different aspects of field boundaries from their place in the landscape to hedges and dry stone walls. Each booklet is full of practical hints and facts: for example, No. 6 on gates, pillars and posts gives a history of iron gates and stone pillars and a description of gates or pillars peculiar to particular parts of the country. At a time when we are being urged to take a holistic approach to our heritage which includes the environment, it is welcome to see DANI taking the initiative in this area and we would hope that everyone living in the country reads these booklets.

McBride, Doreen, *Ceri the Celtic Cow*, (Adare Press, 1992)

With the importance of cultural heritage in schools at present it is welcome to see a local publisher producing a book such as this for use in the classroom. While the style and layout of the book are good, with the reservation that a larger page would have been desirable—it is easy to read, the cartoons are fun, and so on—, there must be some reservations about the content. One cannot expect that recent scholarship on the Celts and their civilisation should be known to everyone, and neither this review nor Ms. McBride's book is the place to discuss it, yet I think that in trying to be simple to read her book results in being simplistic. For example not all cows on Celtic times "had red ears and a white body." Such animals in Celtic mythology were rare and regarded as being devine or of the Other World, and while certain Celts at certain times did behead their dead enemies, I am not aware of any reference in the texts to them "using the heads as footballs." Such stereotyping is to be regretted.

This is not to say that the book is not a useful introduction to the notion of the Celts in Ireland and could certainly be a good starting point for any school project on them, but there is also much in it that is speculative and misleading. Should this book be used in the classroom, it would be better in the hands of a teacher who already knows about Celtic culture and history. Indeed a bibliography for teachers would have been a useful inclusion.

Tony Canavan

McIlrath, R.H., *Early Victorian Larne*, Braid Books, 1991 pp. 136, ISBN 1-873401-06-X. £6.95 (incl. p & p). Available from the author, 14 Curran Road, Larne, Co. Antrim BT40 1BU.

From the point of view of the limited time-scale and geographical focus, early Victorian Larne may not spring to mind as a subject which could support a book extending to almost 140 pages. However, Hilbert McIlrath has proved otherwise, drawing upon a wide variety of referenced source material to produce what must be one of the best and most thorough Ulster local histories to appear in recent years. The author's starting point is the accession of Queen Victoria, finishing approximately thirty years later with an account of the first unsuccessful attempt to establish a regular ferry between Larne and Stranraer. Chapters are not presented chronologically, but rather as a series of separate essays on specific topics including, economy, churches, work-house and living in Larne. Wry humour is evident throughout, from the observance that the Queen-Empress never actually found the time to call in on Larne, to the recording of a contemporary theory that industry in 'Sleepy Larne' was blighted by a mysterious gas emitting from the mud banks exposed at low tide in Larne Lough. The reader may judge for him or herself the pace of life in Larne from the title of the town's local newspaper: the *Larne Monthly Visitor*.

I found the chapter on the newly established local workhouse both balanced and colourful, not least through the re-telling of the resignation of the Workhouse Master following a two or three-day wake (nobody could remember how long it lasted) for one of the inmates, when candles burned throughout the night. In describing quite graphically the harsh and regimented system which the Poor Law Guardians were required to enforce, McIlrath makes the telling point that tyranny as well as liberty requires eternal vigilance. Drawn from their local community, the Guardians were not always up to rigourous enforcement. Local historians in general would do well to look at the actuality and practice of life in their local workhouse, which was run by local people.

It is a theme of this book, that, without the benefit of a local gentry, the communities living in Larne quietly got on with their lives and the angry community faultlines evident in other areas of Ireland did not come to surface in Larne. However life outside the Workhouse was not always orderly, and the author was clearly outraged, even at a distance of one hundred and fifty years, by the sentencing of seven local men to only two years imprisonment for the multiple rape and murder of a local woman. This contrasted with ten years transportation received by two other men at the same court for the theft of a dozen pairs of socks. Also beneath the surface tranquillity, were the various strands of Presbyterianism indulging in internecine squabbling – or rather their respective clergy did. The principal combatants were the orthodox William Molyneaux and the non-subscribing Classon Porter. The wealth of written source material left by the latter gentleman has been made good use of by the author, who exhibits hints of sympathy towards the scholarly Porter rather than the bombastic approach of Molyneaux. This impression is enhanced by the reprinting of the sniffy put-down by the *Belfast Weekly News* of the practice by orthodox Presbyterian ministers, including the Rev. Molyneaux, of accepting honorary doctorates awarded by American universities.

The above is but a scant selection of topics covered in this book, many of which will be of interest to readers whose interests are not necessarily Larne centred. This is particularly so for the transport section, with the accounts of the initial disappointments which accompanied the introduction of both rail and sea ferry transport which today are so important to the town. Even the famed Antrim Coast Road proved to be an initial disappointment as a tourist attraction. All in all, Mr. McIlrath has set a standard which other local historians will find difficult to equal.

R.H. Foy

McKinstry, Robert, et al. (compilers), *The Buildings of Armagh*, (Ulster Architectural Heritage Society, 1992)

This is an excellent illustrated guide to the City of Armagh and its buildings. A street by street catalogue of the city, it describes the buildings – from unprepossessing terraced houses to the magnificent cathedrals – and their history. For any student of architecture or of the cathedral city this book will be of great value. For those not familiar with architectural terms a good glossary is provided, while the photographs and plans are a good guide to how the city once looked. Whether sitting in your armchair or walking its streets, this book is an essential guide to Armagh.

Streetnames: Guidelines / Sráidainmneacha: Treoirlínte – An Coimisiún Logainmneacha (The Placenames Commission) 1992. IR£1.00

Although intended for use in the Republic only, this guide published by An Coimisiún Logainmneacha in association with local authorities, will be of interest to anyone concerned with the continued use of traditional and historic place-names in Northern Ireland. The Guide gives a list of translations of basic generic terms such as Alley (Scabhat), Bridge (Droichead), and even more exotic ones like Mardyke (Mairdíog) or Penthouse (Díonteach). There are also lists of common elements in street names like the names of trees, saints, etc.

The official attitude in the book is one that many would like to see adopted in Northern Ireland. In the preface, the Minister for the Environment, Michael

Smith, says "Placenames have important functions both as links between the people of Ireland and their physical environment today and as links between them and former generations... But is is also necessary to attend to the dynamic aspect of the naming of new roads, streets and districts in the country's towns and cities, and to ensure that the new names relate to the physical environment and local hsitory." In an official circular sent out by the Department of Local Government (quoted on p. 13-14), local authorities are advised that were historic local names have fallen into disuse "through failure to give these names to the roads and streets of the newly developed area [that] historic placenames in these areas should be given a new lease of life by being assigned to the new roads and streets and that they should not be suppressed in favour of other names which have no local connotation...local authorities, therefore, [should] make a special effort to ascertain the traditional names associated with each area being developed with a view to their use in the naming of roads and streets." If such an attitude were adopted by our local authorities then we would see the continuation of our own Ulster names and an end to the flood of names such as Lancastrian Court and Dakota Avenue.

Tony Canavan

The Navan Fort Development

The Navan Centre will be open next summer and will tell the story of Navan Fort, the Ancient political, spiritual and mythological capital of Ulster.

Should any historical society wish to be updated on the plans for the Centre, Navan at Armagh would be pleased to do so.

Contact:
Mr. Paul Mullan
Marketing Manager
Navan at Armagh
Palace Lodge, Palace
Demesne, Armagh BT60 4EL
Tel: (0861) 525550